KATHY TUCCARO

Imagine... Dream... Belie Chang Kathy Tuccaro

DREAM BIG!

OVERCOMING A LIFETIME OF TRAUMA & ABUSE THAT LED TO DREAMS OF SUCCESS

Dream Big!
Copyright © 2017 by Kathy Tuccaro

Cover Photo Credit: Steve Dodge
Back Cover and Author's Bio: Clara Cecilia Photography

Editors: Diana Kurenoff-McGill
          Vladimir Francois

Tellwell Talent
www.tellwell.ca

ISBN
978-1-77370-069-4 (Hardcover)
978-1-77302-940-5 (Paperback)
978-1-77302-941-2 (eBook)

~ *With insight, sensitivity and passion, Kathy deftly shows you how to awaken your dreams of fulfillment and heal the shame and blame of a co-dependent past.*

Brian South, Author of *Demystifying College Admission: It's Your Choice*

~ *In author Kathy Tuccaro, I have found a like mind, spirit and individual—strong, intelligent, diverse, adaptable, wise, and tried by fire. You will be moved to every emotion possible as she finds her willpower and strength in Dream Big! If you don't read anything else, you MUST READ this book! Tuccaro's story is relatable and real with a victorious outcome of one's ability to overcome through divergent thinking and loving the skin you're in. Santé (Cheers) to you for walking your path, connecting the dots, and finding purpose, my friend!*

Dr. Virginia LeBlanc, Author of *Love the Skin YOU'RE In: How to Conquer Life Through Divergent Thinking*

~ *When you DREAM BIG! you completely demolish the old mindset and build a new one. Kathy Tuccaro, Author of "DREAM BIG!" is THE subject matter expert and has created the new blueprint for unlimited success!*

Glen E Gibbs, Author of *Remodel Your Mindset*

~ *DREAM BIG! Is a must-read for anyone who has experienced trauma or is struggling with abuse. This true story of Kathy's personal struggles will touch your heart and will help you take that first step towards freedom from a traumatic past. You learn how to get back your personal power to realize your full potential-beyond your wildest dreams!*

Sarah Wall, Author of *Life Reboot*

~ *Kathy Tuccaro has the ability to motivate readers, and give them the insights to become more successful in their lives. This book is loaded with ideas that allow yourself to Dream Big! and to do the things you love to do.*

Giovana Vega, Author of *Trading for Success*

~ *Many of want our lives to be different but just don't know how. Enter Kathy and her book DREAM BIG! She shows us the way by reaching deep inside us and unleashing a higher power that can make any dream come true. This book is a winner!*

Reena Dayal, Author of *The Brilliance Quotient*

~ *DREAM BIG is a personal mantra of mine. If you want to learn how to DREAM BIG, you need to read this book. You will definitely uncover how to overcome any trauma and abuse that you may have experienced.*

Pix Jonasson, Author of *Think and Grow Rich After Hours*

For my beautiful and loving daughter Tanis. You have loved me unconditionally throughout all my trials and tribulations. You kept believing in me when I couldn't believe in myself. Thank you for your crazy ways, your zest for life, your beautiful laughter and happy disposition, but most of all...thank you for being you just the way you are! The many precious moments we have shared together are priceless and so important to me.

Always remember, "We are Goats".

DREAM BIG!

OVERCOMING A LIFETIME OF TRAUMA & ABUSE THAT LED TO DREAMS OF SUCCESS

Acknowledgements

This book would not have been possible without help from multiple people in my life. I am not talking just about getting this book to print; I am talking about those who have stood by me through the worst days of my life and still continued to believe in me regardless of their frustration. It was as if they saw in me what I could not see for myself. It is to these wonderful Souls whom I would like to extend a special thank you and recognize the importance of their contribution in my life. I am incredibly grateful to all who have contributed to this book.

First and foremost, I want to thank Paul Ferguson, the mine manager who started the pilot project with Women Building Futures. Without his dedication to helping women get involved in the trades, I wouldn't have been able to change my life in such a drastic way. It is also thanks to him that I had the chance to start a boot recycling program at work. The company makes sure boots are delivered when I need them, and it is only because of his understanding of the importance that this program continues. Paul is also responsible for this book cover because of his vision for the message this book contains. He understood the importance of depicting dreaming big on a grand scale; the truck represents just that! He advocated for the picture as the cover because he understood the initial impact that it will have on people who are looking to change their lives. No dream is too big to dream or envision. He also allowed the training department to take time out of their busy schedules to have a mini photo session which is not an easy task in the middle of a busy mine.

I also want to thank Jeff Butters, Myles Sandberg, Gary Butters, Dan Loose from the training department and the beautiful Sue-Ellen Moore for trying so hard to get these pictures to the right people. Steve Dodge from training for the initial picture of the cover; thank you! I will never forget that day as it was a crucial moment in time; a day that has changed all my tomorrows indeed.

I need to extend a huge thank you to my husband Roland Tuccaro; my Ebenezer, my rock. Without him standing at my side as solid as he is, I would have faltered for sure. This incredible man stood beside me during the worst days of detoxing from alcohol, in the worst possible condition that I could ever find myself in, full of hallucinations and psychotic episodes. He ran all over with me just to make sure I was ok and that I wouldn't hurt myself running from all the demons I was seeing and believing to be real. I didn't recount any of those in the book because they are too surreal for anyone to believe. Not once did Roland leave my side; nor did he judge me or condemn me. He just loved me through it all. Even when I started this whole book writing project, he has only uplifted and encouraged me to believe I could accomplish many great things. I am forever grateful that he is still around after the craziness I put him through. You are my everything, Roland. Thank you for loving me through the insanity of my journey to healing.

There is a significant number of people to thank and recognize; too many in fact to mention here. Please don't take an omission of your name personally. I have you in my heart and am grateful for all each of you has done in assisting me on my endless journey of healing. I do have to mention my friend Don Schon because he stood by me during the many years of being so very lost before I ever even knew about recovery. He kept a basement suite apartment just for me for the many times I would call him and tell him I was in a mess...again! He would just laugh and get the apartment ready for me free of charge. I would pay him when I could...which wasn't very often, if ever. He assisted me too many times to count regardless of what situation I found myself in; I can't possibly thank him enough for it. Your helping me through my darkest days is priceless, Don. I hope you know that.

Kathy Noury, my best friend growing up was my light in a dark world! Your beautiful long, golden braids getting stuck in the motor of the go-kart will forever be imprinted in my mind...also the melting chocolate ice cream cone all over the back seat of Grandma's new car. Priceless moments indeed! I love you my friend.

I have to mention my dear friend Denis Hebert from Montreal, who helped me through some crazy difficult times when I was 18-21. His friendship saved me many a time and I am truly grateful for his laughter and genuine care for me. His listening skills and ability to make me laugh were crucial. Merci Beaucoup!

I need to recognize a very, very important woman in my life who gave me a job when I was at my lowest point and struggling through every single day. Shanaz Amlani, a woman of great love and understanding for the hurting. She saw me through the beginning of my journey where I ended up homeless, through to this day. She was there every step of the way lifting me up when I was down, encouraging me when I needed it, and assisted me always with some part-time work in whatever form that took. She loved me through the rough days and today walks beside me in all that I do. I love her like no other.

A special great big thank you to Patti James from B Crew at my job. Her constant love and brainstorming sessions with me are priceless! Thank you for lifting me up and teaching me to see my own inner beauty on the days when I can't see it. You are beautiful my friend.

To Diana Kurenoff-McGill for editing this for me and actually liking it...Who could've guessed as we stood in the WBF pit waiting to get on the rock truck for the very first time that we would be working together editing this book? How life changes!

To my mother for always believing in me no matter what, and showing me that if I couldn't find a way to create one! Thanks mom for teaching me to sing HU in times of distress at the age of 14; this literally saved my life on many occasions! Best gift ever!

I need to acknowledge my sisters for fighting for their lives in their own way. They have survived a hell just as bad as mine and maybe even worse...we all have our mountains to climb and they are still taking a step in the right direction every single day. I love you both dearly.

Lastly, I would like to acknowledge all the women who work in the trades and who have overcome seemingly insurmountable obstacles to get where they are today. Fighting for ourselves is the biggest project we will ever undertake. Stand proud wherever you are and keep taking steps to improve your life. Nothing compares to the empowering feeling of accomplishing great things when people have told us we couldn't do it; especially in a trade where men dominate the workforce. You unknowingly inspire many women who are striving to change careers and stand in their own truth. God Bless you all.

Kathy Tuccaro

This book is dedicated to my cousin and best friend growing up

Sylvie Lebrun
February 8, 1968 - February 8, 2010

You will always be in my heart and I will never forget all the tears
and laughter we shared throughout the years. I love you.

Also to my long-time friend and confidante

Jacqueline Anne Miller
October 24, 1952 – January 2, 2017

She saw me through the roughest as well as the best times of my
life, yet never once judged me or left my side. My only wish is that
she lived to read this book. You will always remain in my heart
Jackie. Love you to bits and back again!

May you both Rest in Peace

Contents

Introduction

Have you ever experienced fear, abandonment, rejection, despair, loneliness, hardships, suicidal thoughts, violence, trauma and pain?

IMAGINE THE POSSIBILITIES IF YOU KNEW HOW TO:

- Skyrocket your self-esteem; set goals and achieve them making your biggest dreams come true
- Overcome your fears and have the courage to take that scary first step towards your dreams
- Set boundaries to release yourself from being a "People Pleaser" and follow your own truth
- Leave the damaged and bruised shell of your past and step into a "new you"
- Break free of the entrapment we set ourselves up with co-dependent behavior
- Find the inner jewels that are hidden deep within your own Soul
- Stand in your own truth and be all that you were meant to Be
- Discover the tools to help you soar to new heights of personal success
- Leave behind all the excess baggage that you may have been carrying around

If you have answered "Yes" to any of the above, then this book is for you!

Everything written in this book is simply from my own personal experiences. The opinions and ideas are mine alone and I have stated what has worked for me as I fought my way through hardships and seemingly insurmountable problems. Some of my insight may be applicable to you, while some may not. Take whatever works for you and apply it in your own life as you see fit. Whatever mistakes are in this book, it is due to my own fault and no other.

This is my story as I have experienced it. Some of it may seem far-fetched, but it only goes to show how mysterious and unpredictable life can be. I have endured a great deal and have chosen to omit details of much of the actual trauma and abuse I suffered. What I do share, however, gives a deep look into my life and may leave you wondering, "How did she get through it all and still smile like she does today?" Know in your heart that you can too. Everybody has a story; mine is really no different than many, many other women out there. There are a lot of women whose story of survival is by far worse than mine. In my future writings, I hope to seek out those stories so I can bring them to light and possibly impact how their stories unfold.

What sets me apart from many is the fire burning deep inside me; it burns brighter than any fire burning around me. I remember once during a beating, my ex stomped on my chest as if he were trying to extinguish a lit cigarette. It was as if he could see the inner fire within my Soul and was trying to put it out. Little did he know, that you can take all my material belongings, you can take my job, you can destroy my self-esteem, you can batter and bruise my body, you can put me down and tear me apart at the very seams, but you will never take away what only I can have. That is the inner light that I have earned over the many years of life and experience! No one can ever take that away from me. What used to be a simple spark fighting to stay alight, has now developed into a full-on flame burning so brightly that even a team of firefighters could not put it out! I don't believe they would even want to, because they see the benefits of the ripple effect of this particular fire. It's one of a kind indeed!

This book is written for all those still suffering, those still amidst the turbulence of windstorms in their lives. I aim to plant a seed that Change is Possible for anyone, anywhere. In whatever miserable circumstances they find themselves in, they can change it if they truly set their mind to it! It will not happen overnight, but if you keep putting one foot in front of the other with your goal in mind, you *will* change your circumstances. I believe this to be true with all my heart and Soul! If the fear of the unknown overrules the passion stirring within your heart, then for sure you will keep feeding that fear and let it prevent you from attaining your dreams. In my case, my overwhelming desire for a better life overpowered any fears and insecurities I had along the way. That burning flame deep inside my Soul simply would not allow me to remain in the circumstances I kept finding myself in throughout my entire life. It was as if I was being guided to take the next step even if I didn't know where I was going. However, at some point you have to make a deep, committed decision that the unfavorable circumstances you find yourself in does not necessarily have to stay that way; commit to do whatever it takes to change it. At any given moment in time, you have the power to say "This is NOT how my story is going to end!" The Universe will help you, but you still have to put in the effort to meet it halfway.

As I recount in Chapter 8, at the very worst time in my life when I found myself at a new level of rock bottom, I was walking the streets for a whole week homeless and depressed beyond tears. In fact, there was no more room for tears, only a deep, dark fog surrounding my every thought that was held tight like prisoner in the depths of despair. My encounter with "Toothless Joe" telling me to enjoy this life; to live it and love it was not an option for me. If he was accepting of his circumstances in life of being homeless, then I sure wasn't! It was as if that slap on the back he gave me was enough to clear the fog in my mind. I looked around at my dismal surroundings and with a sudden, new clarity of mind I thought to myself: *How in the world did I end up here?* It was in that very critical moment in time when I made the committed decision that my current situation was simply NOT how my story was going to end! It just wasn't. No way! I actually stomped my foot and said, "This is NOT my life!" I didn't know where I was going or how I was going to get there; all I knew for sure is what I *didn't* want... being in the company of "Toothless Joe" for the rest of my days. From that moment on, I made the necessary changes and put many incredible efforts into changing my life. Did it all change overnight? Most definitely not! I cried so many tears of frustration and had to overcome an incredible amount of setbacks and obstacles. However, every single step I took, no matter how small it may have seemed at the time, was one in the right direction in getting myself to a better place in life.

Exactly 3 years after my encounter with "Toothless Joe", I found myself standing beside a monster of a truck looking up at in with tears in my eyes again asking myself: "How in the world did I end up here?" There I was in an open pit mine in the Northern Alberta Oil Sands, (seemingly like a different world) staring in complete awe at a truck so big I truly thought I was dreaming! To me, it was as if I was in "Tonka Land," a world of giant machines and ways of life which existed solely on another planet! I never even knew these things existed on earth, and here I was standing beside a truck the size of a house being shown how to drive it! Unbelievable to say the least! The picture on the cover of this book was taken right after that moment. The smile on my face of sheer delight and accomplishment was a very precious moment captured on camera. You can't see the tears of joy and happiness, but they are most definitely there! I was surrounded by a group of people who were all on a tour, and I was the only one crying tears of happiness! A girl who was with me saw the tears and said, "Are you crying?" She laughed at me and looked at me like I was a silly little girl. She had no idea what battles I had fought to get to that moment and what it meant for me to be standing beside the biggest truck in the world! She had no clue about the pain I endured, the obstacles I overcame, the tears of frustration I cried, the hurts I battled, or the overwhelming negative self-limiting beliefs I had to change in my own mind to be able to be standing right beside her. She had no idea the hell I survived and the power it took to be even breathing in that moment. I just looked at her and smiled through my tears of joy because I wasn't about to let anyone take away that moment of accomplishment from me just because they didn't understand. It was my defining moment of Change is Possible!

Exactly 1 year later, I found myself sitting in a mine manager's meeting with the top executives and managers from different departments; I was there as a back-up representative for Occupational Health & Safety (OH&S). As I looked around the room, I recognized a place filled with incredibly smart and powerful people who run the mine, and then there was *me*. I looked around the room and once again thought to myself, "How in the world did I end up here? 4 years ago I was in the company of "Toothless Joe," now I am in the company of Mining Engineers! Unbelievable! How does this even happen?"

Today I sit here writing this book and look back at just how far I have come. I still wonder how my life has managed to change so drastically so quickly. I have spoken on live radio interviews and have appeared on a TV show with regards to my life. I speak at conferences for women, youth as well as at schools. I also travel and offer free self-esteem classes at women's shelters, youth centers and recovery places. All of this is possible because I made a critical decision when standing with "Toothless Joe." I decided how my story would end. This book is only the beginning of a world of wonders to come. What world of wonders awaits you? Know in your heart that Change is Possible and that learning to recognize your own Divinity will be the key to setting your mindset to a different frequency wave.

To all the women in current abusive relationships and who are still suffering today, may this book be a guide to show you that leaving a bad situation is possible. It will take strength and courage beyond words, but ultimately it is *your life* that is at stake. The fact that I am still alive to write this is purely a miracle from God. I should have been dead 10 times over already, but I survived.

My hopes for you as you read this book is that you will take the time necessary to look at your life and re-evaluate what is important for you. Who do you surround yourself with? Are they draining life from you? Or, are they lifting you up when you are down? These are important questions to ask when we are facing change. Where am I going? How am I going to get there? How can I help myself today? Remember...what you tolerate will only continue. So, I ask you: Will today be the day that you make the committed decision to change? Are you ready to commit yourself to changing the circumstances in your life that you don't like? Will today be the day that you say "Enough is enough!"?

I am sure you will experience many emotions as you read along and although it will touch your heart, it is meant to spark and ignite a possible change in your own life. Go deep within yourself and see what is there hiding beneath the many masks you may wear. Go to the true source of all love; it lays within your own heart. This is where the Holy Spirit resides and It will guide your every step if only you would let it. Join me as I walk you through my journey from trauma to triumph and help you start along on your own journey of success!

Kathy Tuccaro

"Love is like a slow, consuming fire, which starts in the center of man's heart and slowly moves outward, destroying all that is in its path. Nothing can stop love, and even when it appears to be quenched, it will break out somewhere else. So it is with freedom. Love comes first in the heart, and with the development of love then ye get freedom; and with the freedom one gets all truth. Love is the essence, spirit, soul and life of all that exists or appears to exist, itself unchangeable and immortal."

~Paul Twitchell~
~Stranger by the River~

Chapter 1:

DOG HOUSE RULES

Fear:

A distressing emotion aroused by impending danger, evil, pain, etc., whether the threat is real or imagined; the feeling or condition of being afraid. Synonyms: foreboding, apprehension, consternation, dismay, dread, terror, fright, panic, horror, trepidation, qualm[1].

Franklin D. Roosevelt said in his inauguration speech on March 4th, 1933 "There is nothing to fear but fear itself." I see it from a different perspective. My very first emotion was fear, and with good reason. As a child, fear altered the very core of my being. Through the eyes of a child, fear is real and all-consuming. Fear ruled my entire being for most of my life. Fear paralyzed me into inaction until the day I realized that unless I overcame it, I would continue to rotate on the same wheel of life and not get anywhere. It was only in a single moment of clarity that I could decide that I would no longer continue to suffer in silence and let fear prevent me from living a life I was dreaming so desperately of having. I wanted a good life more than I was afraid of it, so I did whatever it took to change my situation. I followed my inner voice and took that ever so scary first step into the deep unknown.

---

1   www.dictionary.com/browse/fear

My journey into fear started when I was a toddler. It was dark when I was awoken by a big hand covering my mouth and partially covering my nose, making it impossible to breathe, almost suffocating me. All I saw was a darkened face and a voice whispering for me to be quiet. Intense fear trickled through my veins at the speed of electricity. I felt him on me but I couldn't cry out so I put myself into a deep blackout so I didn't have to live through it and remember it. I never spoke a single word until after I was 4 years old; it's as if the abuse I was subjected to and the hand that was constantly covering my mouth was an indicator for me not to speak. This affected me through every moment in my sleeping and waking dreams, and it's always been as if I never had a voice in my own movie called life. Until now.

My father left when I was 6 months old and my mother was left with 3 small children to care for by herself. So, I was put in the care of a supposedly kind and caring family to watch over me. If only my mother knew what really was going on, I know she wouldn't have left me there. When she remarried and came to get me from them, the fear didn't subside due to the sheer size of my new stepfather who was 6'2 and weighed 250lbs. His hands were the size of my head and his booming voice resonated throughout eternity is seemed. We lived in a small town called Ponteix, in Saskatchewan and by all standards, appeared to be a normal, happy family, one that the whole community envied and aspired to be. Little did they know what went on behind closed doors; sadly those doors held way more horror than the one I'd just left.

My mother had no idea she married a monster, who would soon show himself in all aspects of our lives. He officially adopted us at marriage and this by right made the situation much more difficult for my mother to handle. He ruled the house with an iron fist and leather belt to go with it. We endured many belt lashings, extreme verbal abuse and severe punishments that were unbearable. For example, we were made to kneel in the corner with our arms held straight out horizontally and kept that way. When our arms would tire and started to fall to our sides, he smacked us across the head and screamed at us to raise them again. He quietly and slowly paced behind us, watching like a hawk; we were his prey. The seconds ticked by endlessly and the pain was excruciating, but we had no choice as the fear of the consequences was completely debilitating and all-consuming. Normal living in the house was not possible; we continuously walked on egg shells as his rage was terrifying. We dared not speak and we barely breathed out loud in fear of wakening the beast. His complete power and control over the lives of my mother and us three girls gave him a sense of being King of his castle, and we being the dirty rascals. He truly enjoyed holding authority over everyone who surrounded him and his sheer size helped him accomplish that goal easily. We were simply unable to stand up to him and lived in a constant fear.

On one particular day and for no particular reason, he thought it would be funny to light my sister's flannel pyjamas on fire. I was going up the stairs and could see the living room where my sister, mother and step-father were. He took a match and lit her on fire while laughing hysterically. The flames took on a life of their own as they leapt up her pyjamas. She was screaming, I was screaming and so was my mother. But he sat there and laughed as if it were the funniest thing in the world! Time stopped for me as my world seemed to go by in second by second intervals. I was immobilized with fear watching my poor sister burn. I couldn't breathe; I was completely paralyzed. Finally, at the last second when the flames were at her midriff and began to burn her long, blond hair did he decide to put it out while yelling at her to stop screaming and to quit being such a baby. I couldn't move as I watched the scene below me, transfixed by the demonic and sadistic laughter he belted out as he put the flames out. It is an image that is stamped in my mind to this day.

Fear took on a whole new meaning when the neighbor boys lured me into the garage of their home across the street and tied me to a chair. I was 6 and completely unaware of the danger that was waiting for me so close to home. I remained tied to that chair in the dark, damp garage for the afternoon while they took turns hitting me, pinching me, touching me in private places and mocking me. I was laughed at, spit on, slapped, kicked and my clothes were torn while they attempted to put things where they didn't belong. The harder I cried, the harder they laughed and hit me. They finally let me go when their mother called them in for supper. They threatened to do it again but worse if I told anyone what happened that afternoon. As I ran down the driveway, they laughed and threw rocks at me like I was target practice. When I arrived home, my step-dad took me upstairs and gave me a good lashing with the belt for lying to him about the blood and torn clothes. He was positive I was making that whole story up and called me a filthy little liar. The more I insisted that the story was true, the harder he hit. Eventually, I just admitted that I was lying just so he would stop hitting me. To this day, I have never been able to date anyone with blond hair and blue eyes because of those boys. It's as if I associate the two when it really isn't that way, but that's how my mind works. Thankfully we moved shortly after that, so I didn't have to fear going outside anymore.

We moved to a tiny village called Langbank, Saskatchewan lost amidst the wheat fields where life did not get any better. The trauma in the house only escalated and so did the loneliness and despair I felt.

When trying to do homework, he would stand behind us and if we got an answer wrong, we would be hit in the head and told that we were stupid and useless. Try to concentrate after that; the sheer fright of getting the answer wrong would paralyze us into inaction. The violence was horrific and he would destroy everything in the house or throw whatever was on the supper table or whatever was in the fridge at us. I lost count how many times I went to bed with no supper.

I am left-handed and my sister is right-handed. So, at the dinner table, our elbows would knock as we ate, thus bringing up arguments between the two of us. We both would be stabbed in the hand or forehead with his fork for the interruption and sent to bed without eating. The sheer fright of hearing footsteps going down the hall to my sister's room almost every night was enough to make us want to throw up. We knew a little bit of what was going on because of his intense possessive attraction to her. We were completely helpless in doing a single thing we were so afraid. For the most part, I would only have to take baths with him and shower with him as well.

He would have me sit on his knee and touch me up and down, when I would tell him to stop, he would laugh and say I had nothing to touch anyways...but he would still keep doing it. He especially despised me out of us three girls and I got the brunt of his disgust and rage. The verbal attacks were traumatizing and left a huge impression on me for my entire life. I had no self-worth and felt stupid and ugly. I kept trying to win his love and attention to no avail. Finally, I just gave up and found the only place of safety I knew...the doghouse. This is where the theme "Dog House Rules" was founded. I would spend hours there dwelling in the love of my dog Sheba; it was all I had. Nobody would think about or care where I was, and it was there that I felt safe. My poor mother was having a difficult time functioning due to all the abuse, and did the best she could with what she had. When it came to the dog house, I had made up the rule that only love and happiness was allowed in; no anger, violence, sickness of any kind was allowed to cross the threshold of the dog house door. I would bring in my lunch and share it with the dog, so I could just sit quietly for a while and talk to God asking Him why life was like this. Where are you, God? How could you let this happen? I had long conversations with God and was looking for answers that I didn't get. I just didn't understand anything and was so confused about life. I was desperately hurt and alone as I searched for answers to life at such a young age. The only thing I knew to be true was the love from the dog. He was all I had and cherished those quiet moments in the dog house; that is until the day my step-dad took the dog out back and shot him. The complete devastation by his action changed me and I vowed to get away from this chaos one day soon. It was at the age of 7 when I started running away; and continued to run my entire life. When something became too traumatic in life, I would just leave. It was my solution to everything. I would gladly drop whatever I was doing and run away from all my problems.

I truly was alone from that moment on as my two sisters had a deep bond and I most definitely was not included, which left me even more alone with my misery. We lived in terror of every little thing. Fear...so much fear, unhappiness, loneliness, misery and despair. My mother had withdrawn into a deep depression and was unable to cope with the unbearable situation and not knowing how to get out. The pain, the violence, and the trauma were too much to handle. She ended up in the hospital for a month trying to get better and figure out how in the world we would get out of this situation because in 1980 there weren't many options available. When my mother spoke to the priest about the situation, he flat out told her that she married the man, therefore had to endure whatever came her way. She kept trying to find ways to get out because she soon found out that he was molesting my oldest sister, and that his brother and his father had done the same. Even though she was terrified of him because she bore the brunt of the violence, she finally went to Social Assistance and began talking to someone there. An investigation was conducted and some people came to the house to verify what was going on. He admitted to the investigators what he was doing, but the only thing that happened was that we were put on a train back to Quebec and left him behind. No charges were ever laid against him. He just went on with life hurting God only knows how many more people and how many other little girls. Where is the justice in that?

There are too many instances and moments in my life where fear ruled my entire being. I have spent my entire life living in fear. I was afraid to speak because every time I opened my mouth, I was told what I said was dumb, stupid and a waste of air so it would be better if I just didn't speak. I was afraid of the consequences if I did speak or act in the wrong way; I was almost afraid to breathe because fear was so engrained in my life. Later in life, I was afraid to speak my mind for fear of ridicule and violent outbursts from whoever was standing in front of me; I was afraid to ask questions in school; afraid to talk about the dysfunction going on at home; afraid to talk about the sexual abuse that was going on; I was afraid of everyone and everything around me. I kept all of my questions and concerns to myself believing that everything that happened to me was my fault because I was stupid, ugly and unbearable to be around. I believed this as a small child! Imagine how my teenage years reflected this? My adult years?

This way of thinking affected all my decisions, my choices, my thought patterns in all that I did. It took a long time for me to unravel the mess and re-train my brain into thinking positive things about myself. Fear ruled my world for so long, that to learn to live in peace and comfort took a huge effort on my part, and demanded constant re-enforcement and reminders that I was stronger than anything that came my way. Fear affected every cell in my being down to the very core of who I am today. I still struggle with it but have learned over the years how to face whatever it is that I fear, and stand strong in the face of adversity. I simply will NOT let fear rule my life any longer. That ship has long since sailed! I had to learn to talk myself through situations that came up and attempted to cripple me into inaction. I would be the only person to help myself through it because the sad reality is that people have their own problems and their own lives.... so who really cares? The same goes for anyone reading this book. You and you alone will be the Master and Commander of your own ship. Where it sails is completely up to you. Are you going to sail in a continuous circle and end up sucked in by the whirlpool and sink deep into unknown waters? Or are you going to make a decision about exactly what direction you want your ship to sail, and keep it going that way? What comes and goes in your life will be determined solely by what you continue to allow. The only way to change is to take that very first step and honestly look at yourself. You have to ask yourself those hard questions and answer them truthfully. What *really* is going on with you when it comes to Fear?

As much as there are several potential triggers to your fear, there are also as many types of fears. However, they can be categorized into three basic fears: external, internal, or subconscious. Among the three, the subconscious and internal type of fear are most difficult to find treatment to because the person must take the initiative to recognize the source of fear and take necessary steps to overcome it. Recognizing the category in which your fears fit into will help you know how to deal with it.

External Fear: Among the types of fear, this one is the easiest to diagnose and manage. It is similar to phobias wherein an outside source elicit a degree of internal fear or any manageable level of anxiety. For example, fear of spiders or fear of heights are among the most common phobias that several people share. A feeling of fear, anxiety or discomfort is experienced by the person with that particular fear when the situation confronts them with those triggers. Since the source of fear is easier to identify, then one can easily look for alternative ways in which to confront that trigger and overcome fear.

Since external fears are often caused by negative experiences in the past involving those external sources of fears, you can adapt some techniques that will help you understand the reality of the situation. Hypnosis or some other psychological methods are employed in order to erase any previous negative associations with these objects or creatures that elicit fear.

Internal Fear: This type of fear is closely associated with low levels of self-esteem or confidence. But like with external fear, the triggers are coming from an outside source and yet it produces a negative emotion. This trigger will then produce internal reactions or fears such as self-doubt or questioning one's capability to do something. Most often, when people begin to question their own abilities, failure is inevitable. This type of fear often impacts one's ability to interact with the social environment. If you want to conquer internal types of fear, you often have to go back at your childhood years wherein character development is at its peak. This is the stage in people's lives wherein they build characters and develop fears. Some people seek professional help that enables them to adapt a new perspective in life and change any behaviors that produce such insecurities and fears.

Subconscious Fear: This type of fear is produced by accepted beliefs in your mind that serve to limit your potentials and worse, could end up in self-sabotage. This one is somewhat associated with the internal type of fear wherein you have the tendency to question your capacity to achieve something. Thus, the tendency for self-doubt and negative self-talk. This one requires you to take active steps towards reversing those beliefs and enable you to maximize your potential.

Goals to Overcome Your Fears: One of the many reasons why people neglect the need to overcome their fears is the lack of motivation. Therefore, setting goals will help increase the desire to manage and overcome your fears. Aside from that, this will enable you to take careful methods toward your goal and provide a sense of direction. One benefit you can get from it is that aside from getting rid of your fears, it offers more focused direction in your everyday living as opposed to not having a clear idea of what you want to do in life. Setting goals as motivation to overcoming your fears will also enable you to have a bigger grasp at the need to fight your fears as an opportunity to grow and delimit yourself.

Take a moment and look at your life, take stock and reflect on the moments that have changed your perception of fear. Today I understand fear because I met it head on and can honestly say as an adult, there are some life threatening situations out there where fear is appropriate due to the situation at hand. However, when Franklin D. Roosevelt said: "There is nothing to fear except fear itself." in many cases this is also the truth. Fear will grow into whatever you keep feeding it. Just like anything else in life, what you focus on is what you will attract. If all you do is think about how afraid you are of something, or that you will automatically fail, then guess what? Your fears might just materialize. Ask yourself are you afraid of failure or of success? What happens is you succeed at something and aren't able to handle it because you don't believe in yourself? My thought has always been: if you feel you didn't succeed; then redefine success. Make it work for you with less expectations attached to it. Everyone has a different definition of failure and success. Simply redefine yours and edit it to suit your needs and not those of society. Make a list of benefits and burdens of both so you can measure just how effective a change in perspectives will help in the long run.

Fear can be a burden that we tend to carry around with us wherever we go, just like excess baggage. Once you face your fear, you will find the energy that fueled it is gone. There is nothing left to give it power. Once you have enough courage to look closely at your fears two things happen: 1) you find that it wasn't so bad after all; you say to yourself,"Really? that was it? Why was I so worried and afraid? 2) you will be able to come to terms with them. In my case, I realized most of the time that the fear I had created in my imagination was just that: my imagination. As I learned to release my old fears and cling onto hope, I started to develop more confidence; I found the courage to try new things because I didn't have fear holding me back. Because the fear was now gone, I was more willing to take chances that I would never in a million years had thought about before. Just like I did leaving a 13-year nursing career to become a Heavy Equipment Operator at 42. Did I have fears? Absolutely! But my desire to change my life desperately overruled any fears I may have had at any given time.

The whole idea of life is to grow spiritually and be better than we were yesterday. Coming face-to-face with ourselves including all our fears, insecurities, and other useless things we drag around with us like luggage that we no longer need, will give you a newfound freedom. If you are able to recognize where the attachment to your fear is, it will help you let it go. You have to find what it is that is holding you to it so intensely. List your fears and all the possible outcomes on a piece of paper. Write down what the *attachment* to the fear is, which is keeping you prisoner to the problem. In writing it down, you start the internal process of releasing it to the Universe. *The key therein lies in learning to be detached to the problem*; and when you are finally able to do this, you will find that you are relieved of its burden. If you are able to look at your problem, face it, look at it from a different perspective and detach yourself from it, you will indeed be free from the fear that binds you to it. It is now my belief that as long as fear does not come into your mind, you will not feed it. The moment fear creeps in and you begin to feed it, you automatically give it power and energy to become a nightmare. Don't let fear control your every thought, action and deed. . Remember that every present thought will transform itself into a future condition, so be careful of too many negative thoughts.

Here's a simple exercise to try: when you start to feel fear creep into your mind, try to replace it with gratitude and love. Shut your mind and open your heart; when you do this, where is there room for fear? Fill your heart centre with love and gratitude and you will see that fear will slowly dissolve. When you are in this state of mind, it becomes easier to focus on a solution to your problem as opposed to shutting down because fear took over. It gives you a better perspective to approach with a heart full of love and gratitude instead of one full of fear. I am not saying this in a life or death situation, it is meant for when fear from insecurity or low self-esteem creeps in, then is the time to fill yourself with love. Just think of someone you love, even a pet, fill your heart center with that image and give yourself time to review your situation with love in your heart instead of fear. Works every single time. Talk yourself through the fear.

What has worked for me in the past when dealing with fear is a simple exercise my mother taught me when I was 14 years old. She taught me how to meditate/contemplate so I could better focus at school. Instead of chanting the age-old word "OM" as you sit cross-legged with your eyes closed, she had me sing the word HU which is an ancient name for God. This powerful word can raise your awareness, help you experience divine love, mend a broken heart, dissipate fear, offer solace during times of grief and bring peace and calm inside you so you can better deal with daily life. It is pronounced like the word hue and sung in a long drawn out breath H-U-U-U-U-U. Take another breath and sing HU again. Continue this for up to twenty minutes. When you sing HU with a feeling of love, it will gradually open up your heart to love instead of fear.[2] It has worked for me in countless situations when I was in danger and scared out of my mind. It soothed my inner fright and helped me see a different perspective of the situation. It also gave me courage to pick myself up when I was down and work through the long, dark nights of Soul. When you are full of fear and uncertainty try this simple exercise and you will gradually see a huge difference in yourself. The HU is a powerful, spiritual sound; it can start changes to happen that are best for us, which are sometimes totally different than we expected. Try this for 20 min a day morning or night, or whenever you feel the need to. I have shared this exercise with many and they also have claimed this powerful word has helped them achieve inner peace over turmoil. I sing it quietly or aloud when I drive, when I am confronted with an angry person, or with a difficult situation, when I am anxious about something or when I simply need to relax and find inner peace and comfort. I also sing it when I am filled with love and gratitude for this gift of life. Fill yourself with love instead of fear and you will start to see a difference in the way life unfolds for you. Never let your fear decide your fate, because on the other side of fear lies FREEDOM!

When fear is the dominant force in your life, it takes away all joy of living in your day to day life.

~Harold Klemp~

STOP AND REFLECT

1. What 3 fear factors in your upbringing has affected you as an adult today?

   _____

   _____

   _____

   _____

2. How has fear of failure held you back in your life? What about fear of success?

   _____

   _____

   _____

   _____

3. How is fear holding you back from being yourself, from following your own dreams or from the pressure of what others might think?

   _____

   _____

   _____

   _____

4. What could you accomplish if you weren't afraid of anything? Take fear out of your vocabulary. How does this change your insecurities? What if you can actually do this?

_____

_____

_____

_____

_____

_____

_____

_____

5. Have you ever considered writing out your utmost deepest fears in a letter then burning it afterwards? It works wonders! Try it sometime as writing/journaling is a tool for healing the hurting Soul. It can become a release for words you are unable to express verbally. Write below all the things you are afraid of in life; then try to find a solution for how to face that fear and banish it from your life. It will empower you beyond measure!

_____

_____

_____

_____

_____

_____

Chapter 1: DOG HOUSE RULES

Chapter 2

SANDS OF TIME

LONELINESS:

Affected with, characterized by, or causing a depressing feeling of being alone; lonesome[3].

I can be surrounded by 1000 people yet still feel alone. I can be at work amidst 100 of the same people every day and still feel alone. I can be all by myself yet feel surrounded by the company of 1000 Angels and am fulfilled. How can this be?

Loneliness causes much despair in people all around the globe. I believe it is the most common form of mental health problem in us all. We seek the comfort and love of another human being. It is instinct to be with others and feel loved and appreciated by someone. To live a life full of dejection, rejection and being utterly alone in this sad, crazy world is, I believe, to be the most challenging of all wars that life throws on our path. I believe that in order to achieve personal mastery, we need to go through every test that life gives us and learn to pass them. Otherwise, the tests will keep coming back until you've kicked its ass and stomped on it! How hard it is to overcome that feeling

---

3   www.dictionary.com/browse/loneliness

of loneliness and desperation at Christmastime when everywhere you look you see people buying gifts and throwing parties for family gatherings. When you are broke and all alone, cold and homeless, perhaps. Every single human being has this feeling at some point in their life whether they want to admit it or not. It is part of human nature. Loneliness is powerful contributor in the lives of the hurting when it comes to poor coping skills and addictive behaviours. In my case, I grew up extremely lonely, lost in my thoughts. In order to keep my sanity and save myself from being admitted into an asylum, I had to create "Kathyland," a beautiful and safe place where nothing can hurt me.

When my mother was finally able to get away from our crazy step-father, we ended up in Malartic, Quebec; my mother's home town where all her family resided. We got there with only the clothes on our back and what little support her family could give us. It was 1982 and times were extremely tough. My loneliness only escalated because we were in a French only community and we only spoke English at the time. So here we are 4 extremely damaged and vulnerable Souls left to fend for ourselves. Unsuspectingly, we became wide open game for all the predators out there. We left an environment filled with rigid rules, violence, fear and hurt, and now all of a sudden we found ourselves in a situation that was the complete opposite; free will and wide open space to do as we pleased. Mom had to work 2 and sometimes 3 jobs to try and support 3 fast-growing teenage girls, so she was barely home, and when she was, she had begun to drink to relax. My two sisters were inseparable, which left me completely alone in our sparsely furnished apartment that had more house plants than actual furniture to fill in the bare areas, and give it an appearance of peace and happiness. I once counted 75 house plants in our small apartment; just watering them was a chore in itself! Our couch was actually 3 old mattresses put on top of one another since we just didn't have money for a real couch. Money was non-existent so we ate a lot of potatoes and macaroni. Mashed potato sandwiches were a regular in my school lunch. In reality, my life was filled with loneliness and desperation, and I was searching for the ever elusive love and attention of my family, which I never did get. Over time however, we became the most popular family in the town and we held many, many parties in our place. It became the local hangout for all the kids in town. We had our own little gang and did what everyone did back in the 80's... party hard! Mom would rather us be at home where she could call and check in on us from work, than to hang around only God knows where and get into all kinds of trouble. It was her way of keeping us safe I guess, and at least she knew where we were and could for the most part reach us when needed.

It is during these trying times at the young age of 12 that I had my first Spiritual Experience. We lived across from a giant cathedral of a church, and from our 2nd story apartment bedroom window I spent hours and hours looking at the majestic beauty of it and wondering about God. I had so many unanswered questions. Where are you God was the biggest of my concerns. In church and at my Catholic School, we learned about God's never -ending love, but as far as I was concerned I had yet to witness or experience it. All I knew was despair, pain and extreme loneliness...there was no love in my world, what was up with that? I called bullshit. Then, the first glimpse of hope came to me in a dream so real I was sure it had to be true! I was dreaming one night that I was sitting with my head out the window pondering the existence of God while staring at the giant cathedral outside, when Jesus and 12 Angels floated down on puffy, white clouds and landed on the front lawn of the Church. The incredible colors of sparkling blue, yellow, oranges and pinks will be imprinted on my mind forever! The grandness of the enormous wings on the backs of the Angels and the music that enveloped them all truly was heavenly! With a hint of exasperation I cried, "There you are! Where were you? I have been looking all over for you!" I went running down the stairs as fast as I could towards the incredible sight of Jesus and the 12 Angels. He was smiling gently and said, "Come Kathy, Come!" I ran as fast as I possibly could, still miffed that he had taken his sweet time to come to get me, but ever so grateful that he finally did show up. My running slowed down to a trot as I suddenly noticed the air around me was dark and thick like a dense fog threatening to swallow me whole. I came to a complete stop as I began to notice something strange going on; everyone on the street all around me was frozen in time. Frozen in motion, unable to speak or move; just like in a movie when time stops. I was the only one moving towards Jesus and the Angels. My friends and family couldn't see the beautiful, majestic sight that I was seeing. Or if they did, they couldn't move in the direction of it whatsoever. Confused, I looked at Jesus questioningly, and with the saddest look I had ever seen filled with such deep compassion, He replied, "It is not their time yet; they are not ready! But you are Kathy, my little one...so come!" Appalled at having to leave them behind in the darkness and emptiness of the world, I almost reluctantly climbed into Jesus arms and up we went into the Heavens above, Angels and Divine music all around us. I awoke with the deepest satisfaction of having all my questions finally answered. I rushed to the window to see if I could still see Jesus and all the beautiful Angels on the lawn of the church, but was met only with the cold hard reality of ugly traffic and nasty, northern Quebec weather. I looked up to the sky and thanked God for the confirmation that He did in fact exist and that I truly was loved and never would be alone again. This dream experience soothed me through the difficulty of day-to-day struggles. Life didn't appear so dark anymore as I kept reliving my moment with Jesus whenever I needed it. It soothed my inner fears until another hurdle came my way that would bring my pain and suffering to a whole new level.

It came in the form of my very first boyfriend who was very charming at first, and made me laugh like crazy in a world filled with despair. Having gotten lost in the problems and dysfunction going on at home, I had no one to really talk to. Although, I did have a crazy best friend who remained like a burst of sunshine and whose friendship I valued dearly. Her name was Kathy as well. Her nickname was "Tootsie" therefore my nickname became "Tootsie" as well. She had beautiful long golden braids that went down to her backside, a face full of freckles, a loud vivacious laugh, and lordy...was she ever full of mischief! She helped me keep my sanity through tough times. Tootsie, you will always be remembered and cherished for saving me from despair. She became my only source of escape in a dark and dreary world called my life. But even with her, I could not speak of what I was living with my boyfriend who was pushing me and forcing himself on me in ways I was not prepared to have at 14 while he was 17. His hands were everywhere and I felt constant bile in the back of my throat as I just wasn't wanting it to happen. Although I kept repeating no and telling him to stop, he just wouldn't take no for an answer. I felt forced out of sheer fright because he would leap into fits of rage and scream at me, just like my step-dad used to. In the next instant he would cry and tell me he loved me and would never hurt me if only I would do this for him. I was paralyzed with fear of the consequences of refusing and terrified of his raging outbursts. I had no voice and ultimately felt like I had no other choice in the matter.

Completely immobilized by panic and fear of violent consequences, he forced himself on me and hurt me telling me all the while that I would love it. I didn't know how to get out of the situation, so I let him have his way rather than fight a beast I knew I would lose to anyway. I endured 6 long months of this until he finally tired of me and found a new girl to harass. I then had to endure his constant mocking me with his friends and saying horrible things about me as I walked down the street; it was a very small town after all and really nowhere to hide seeing as we all hung around the same people.

I thought things would get better when my mom announced that my real father was coming for a visit. This would be my first time seeing him and I was so longing for his love and approval; hoping he would whisk us away to live a loving and happy life. Sadly this wasn't the case; he took us out for dinner, gave us a cold speech on not doing drugs and dropped us off. He completely ignored me like I didn't even exist! I was so very hurt and devastated by his rejection; this has stayed with me until late adulthood. Not being wanted or loved by your step-father who cursed every move you made; to be completely pushed away by your sisters because you were a pain in the ass bother; ignored by your tired mother because she was so busy trying to survive, put food on the table and provide for 3 growing teenage girls by herself; and now to be coldly shoved away by the one person I wanted so desperately to love me...my very own father who had abandoned me at 6 months old. Here he was abandoning me again because he now had another family that he chose over us. This scarred me deeply and I cried many a tear over that loss. I felt completely worthless, ugly, and unlovable. I cried for Jesus and his Angels to come back and get me, and kept watching the front lawn of the Church for his return, but had to settle for the lasting memory of it. I felt like the ugly duckling that just wanted to fit in and be loved. Through this difficult time, I started to bond with my cousin Sylvie, whose world wasn't really better than mine. She had long black hair with bangs covering her nose, she wore dark clothes that where 3 sizes too big so she could hide behind them. She had the sleeves cover her hands and you could see her scowling all the time. She was filled with misery and let the whole world know it! We truly made an unlikely friendship, but my main mission in life at that point was to make her laugh, because when she did....boy oh boy! Her smile lit up the room and so did her laughter! Finding ways to make her smile took me out of my own misery and gave me a purpose in life. Even though life was hard, I just couldn't let her go through life hating the world and everyone in it, so I did my very best to show her love and happiness. Even though we were two completely different individuals, we became the best of friends and were inseparable until life took us our separate ways. Later in life, I would constantly play tricks on her like moving everything around in her cupboards and shelves. She would get so mad at me for messing up her perfectly arranged house because of her need for order in her life. It was too much for me, so I would mess it up just to bug her. I do miss her.

Not long after I had begun to heal from the abrupt rejection from my own father who chose his new family over us, the family who had fostered me until I was 4 years old, contacted my mother wanting to see me again. She thought it would be a good idea for me to get to know them again. She said they were rich and would take good care of me if I was good to them. She realized how poor and how hard life was for us and was looking for something better for us all. Her way of thinking was they had taken such good care of me when I was little, they would do the same now that I was 15. She really had no idea of what the family was really like; neither did I as those deep, lost memories only came back through heavy sexual abuse treatment I underwent much later in life. I had no idea of what nightmare I was about to walk into.

Off I went to spend Christmas with them in Red Lake, Ontario with the high hopes in finding a family who would love and appreciate me for who I was. Boy was I ever wrong....From the minute I stepped into that home I knew something was very, very wrong with the family dynamics. It started out with the Greyhound bus losing all my luggage leaving me with absolutely nothing to wear for my two week stay. To top it off, the clothes the youngest daughter gave me were too small, so I had to wear tight fitting clothes that made me look like dessert I suppose. I felt only disdain and unspoken anger amidst the entire family. I wasn't sure what was going on but tried to alleviate the situation with my usually happy disposition. I was frowned upon and left to myself to wonder how I was going to handle 2 long weeks with this very unhappy family. Although they had a nice home with expensive furniture, a dark cloud of misery hung over the entire house. The air, which was underlined with hatred, was dense and thick making breathing difficult. Dinner times were by far the most uncomfortable as conversation was non-existent and daggers were thrown by all who sat there. I felt awkward and out of place even though I desperately wanted them to love me and accept me as their own. It was at these uncomfortable dinners that I understood really quickly that the father had a drinking problem, and the way he was looking at me made me feel as though I was going to be dessert. This is no good I thought to myself; I just want to go home already! I was very shy and quiet but searching for a way to communicate the deep inner love I always held deep inside me. The air in the house became so thick with hatred that I just longed to go home. I truly didn't understand what was going on and tried desperately to make peace within the family. The youngest daughter wanting none of it, went to spend Christmas vacation at a friend's leaving me alone at the mercy of the couple from hell, while the oldest daughter was nowhere to be found. She must've known and left as well.

It was at this vulnerable moment that the father made his intentions towards me known. He started to squeeze my knee and rub his leg on mine underneath the kitchen table at dinner while his wife sat across from him. Shocked and worried, I didn't know how to handle the situation. I wanted to throw up I was so sickened by it. The wife's eyes were like darts loaded with venom waiting to strike when no one was looking, and she frightened the wits out of me! She would be absolutely no help to me or anyone else for that matter. Every evening after dishes she retired to her room, leaving me with this drunken fool of a man who had started to follow me everywhere I went in the house. He started touching me when I was sitting quietly watching TV and looked at me with the eyes of a starving man, which terrified me! Every night he came into my room, and slid under the covers to fondle me. Even when I would tell him to go away and leave me alone, he just wouldn't take no for an answer. I would go sleep on the couch in hopes that he would leave me alone, but to my despair he would come and lay on me there and attempt to have sex with me. I couldn't seem to fight him off. I didn't know how to tell the wife of her husband's roving hands. One night when it got to a point that he was trying to take my pyjamas off, I managed to push him off of me and ran to her room, climbing into bed with her telling her I had a nightmare. I was too afraid to tell her the truth. The next day, he announced that he was putting me on a plane back home. I cried tears of sheer relief and had never missed my dysfunctional family as much as in that very moment. Anything was better than this unhappy family who appeared to be locked in a deep, dark imaginary dungeon of some sort. I couldn't get out of there fast enough! He said he would drop both his other daughter and me at the airport at the same time and I was thrilled to get the heck away from these miserable people under any means necessary. However, this was not to be the case as unbeknownst to me, he had other plans. He sent his daughter on a flight but said there weren't any flights available for me, so he decided to drive me to Thunder Bay and catch a plane from there. Great! Just great! I knew without a doubt that he had other plans for me and getting on a plane in Thunder Bay was not one of them. Dear God help me please!

It was cold, getting dark outside, and a snowstorm was creeping in; just like his hand was creeping up my leg the minute we were alone in the car. Intense foreboding overwhelmed me as I watched him pull out a mickey of whiskey and drink heavily from it. I knew I was in deep trouble and didn't know how to get out of my situation. His hand kept going higher and higher up my thigh until it reached the parting of my legs. Even though I told him to stop it and tried to push it away, he only tightened his grip on my inner thigh to a point of hurting me, and kept it there telling me in no uncertain terms that his hand was staying there whether or not I liked it. Fear raced through my body and paralyzed me into inaction. I was as close to the car door as I possibly could get in hopes he would forget about me, sinking deep into my thoughts as I envisioned many bad scenarios where I would end up losing this fight. Completely frozen with fear and by what the night would hold, I started to pray silently for help.

The foreboding intensified when he pulled over and got a motel room due to the storm, or so he said...yeah right! Did he think I was completely daft? The fear rushed through me like wildfire spreading across a dry field of brush, but I remained unable to utter a single word; I was so alone and afraid. Terrified of the outcome, I didn't know how to get out of this and kept praying and praying as he kept drinking and drinking. I was in an unknown small town in the middle of a blowing snowstorm and it was nighttime. I had absolutely no idea where we were other than a motel room in the middle of nowhere. I needed a miracle and fast!

The moment arrived when he pounced on me like a cat does its prey. His hands, and his hot, disgusting breath were all over me at once. I screamed and tried to push him off but his weight only held me down. He was a big man and at 15 years old, I was no match to fend him off. He started tearing at my pyjamas and managed to get the bottoms off while I tried to fight off his evil intentions, which only seemed to arouse him even more as if he enjoyed the struggle and control over me. Somehow, someway and to this day I still don't know what happened, but in one fell swoop, he flew off of me and landed on the other side of the bed. It was as if someone or something had pulled him off of me; my miracle had just arrived! I have always believed it was Divine Intervention, because I know I sure wasn't strong enough to get this beast of a man off of me like that. In that one second of freedom, I ran to the bathroom and locked myself in with my feet on the sink and my back holding the door. He came flying into the door so hard it almost knocked me off balance, but I was determined to not let him in because the outcome would be a very bad thing for me. Try as he might, he could not break down the door thankfully. (I like to think angels were holding the door shut with me.) I remained in that position with feet on the sink and back to the door for a long time after he stopped pounding on it. Pinpricks ran through my legs as they shook with the weight of my body, but there was no way I was about to let go of the only lifesaving action I had.

He finally let up, and after a while, I could hear him drinking again at the other end of the room. I remained in that position while trying to plan on how to get away from him. The bathroom was located right beside the door, so I counted the seconds and calculated the layout of the room, where my shoes and pyjama bottoms were located; the time it would take to open the door, grab them and run like hell. I waited until I heard him breathe heavily on the bed, and with all the courage I had, I opened the door, grabbed my shoes and pyjamas, and then ran out of the room into the parking lot into a dark and blowing snowstorm. His pretending to be asleep was a ruse on his part, because he came flying after me howling like an enraged beast chasing his escaped prey. Fear was my ammunition and had me running like a deer into the night. I managed to hide between cars in the parking lot until I watched him drive away looking for me. Still in my pyjamas, I went to the front desk to ask the guy who was working for a room key so I could get my clothes, as it was -30 and a really bad snowstorm was blowing. Unbelievably, he wouldn't help me! He said my name wasn't on the roster and he couldn't give me a key. Here I am standing in my pyjamas and running shoes at 15, giving him the name of the man who was attacking me, and he said he wouldn't let me in to get my clothes! Unreal! In a state of shock and numbness, I left and had no idea of what to do. The wind was howling and the snow was blowing heavily all around me in the dark night. I was so completely lost, cold and alone in the middle of nowhere with no help available. I couldn't believe that man would not help me! What was I supposed to do?

I saw a payphone across the street and went to go make a collect call home. My boyfriend at the time, told me to go back and have him call the police, which suddenly made complete sense to me. Why I hadn't even thought of that I don't know...GOD was with me, because as I was crossing the street to go talk to the motel room guy, a police car stopped right in front of me as I was crossing the road. I started crying and told them the whole story. They went to the room and collected all my stuff and we drove around looking for his car which was easy to find at the local bar. I even went into the lobby and pointed him out sitting on a bar stool with a drink in his hand. Back at the police station, they had me call his wife and unbelievingly, she began to screech at me like an old, sickened crow. She was screaming that I was a troublesome little whore and I was trying to lure her husband into my bed. (As if...gross!) She was yelling obscenities so loudly that even the police were taken aback and immediately took the phone away from me to talk to her. In the end, I was put in a foster home for 3 days until I could be put on a flight back to Quebec. No charges were ever laid in this incident, and when I got back home, it was as if it never happened at all. Nothing was ever talked about or even mentioned about it. Personally I didn't care, because I was just so happy to be safe in my dysfunctional home. At least we had love and laughter in our poor home, unlike the intense anger and hatred that I had just left. I was very grateful in fact to have experienced that because it taught me that money doesn't by happiness. I would rather be poor and at least be able to smile and live free than to be trapped in the miserable existence of that family. No thank you! I will keep what I have, because the one thing my mother always insisted is that we have the ability to laugh and love in life, no matter what our circumstances are. She said if ever we lost that, we would lose our sanity in an instant. She would show me people who walked around town with a tight, wrinkled face and stiff walk and tell me I would end up looking like that if I didn't find the ability to laugh and love; I would die a crispy, miserable old woman. Yikes! That's a fate I flat out refused to have.

Loneliness is a powerful thing; it can make a person do things they wouldn't normally do otherwise. Why is this so? I have come to understand that until you are good with yourself first and foremost, loneliness will always come to haunt you. You have to be able to be alone with your thoughts and learn to understand yourself in all aspects. This takes an honest and deep reflection of who you really are; your likes and dislikes. My years of deep and desperate loneliness brought me to a place I never want to go back. I so desperately wanted someone, anyone, to pay attention to me and to love me that I would transform myself into a chameleon so that the person standing in front of me would want me and love me. I could become whoever it was that they wanted me to be at any given time. I felt so ugly and unwanted that I would almost do anything for their friendship. What's even worse, is that I only realized I was doing this much later in life when I finally went to treatment. By then, I was so completely broken that I simply couldn't function any longer and had no idea of who Kathy really was. Life shouldn't have to be like this.

Loneliness can cause depression and bring about addictive behaviours as well. We are geared for social interaction, so when we are alone and start to dwell on our problems, we seek out the company of sometimes not the healthiest of people. We start to settle for less and tolerate more due to our inability to remain alone with ourselves. What I have finally understood is that we are the masters of our own ship and destiny, so we have to take charge of our lives and figure how to change a bad situation into a good one. I personally had zero coping skills or even life skills, so everything I learned was the hard way. This book will hopefully prevent a few people from going down the same path that I did. Many people stay in bad relationships just because they don't want to be alone. Today I see loneliness from a different perspective. I ask myself "Why not?" What is so wrong with being alone? Why don't we use this time by ourselves to re-evaluate what is important to us in life? Why don't we use this time to figure out what we need to do in our lives to make it better? Today, I can stand alone but I am not lonely. I have learned to appreciate whatever precious time given to me and savour every single moment that comes my way whether it's good or bad. What are you doing with the borrowed time that you have?

It took years of fighting my way through the hordes of self-destructive thoughts and long, lonely, dark nights to figure out that I carry the Secret deep within me wherever I go. This Secret is simple: I AM WHO I AM! Just like God told Moses at the Burning Bush on Mount Horeb; I have discovered the "I AM" factor, which helped layout the direction of my life. This factor works like this:

· Tell yourself you are lonely; you will be lonely
· Tell yourself you are ugly; you will feel ugly
· Tell yourself you are fat; you will see yourself as fat
· Tell yourself you are stupid; you will feel stupid
· Tell yourself you are weak and vulnerable; you will be weak and vulnerable
· Tell yourself "I AM Beautiful!" you will feel like a Queen!
· Tell yourself "I AM just right the way I AM" you will be just perfect!

- Tell yourself "I AM SMART" you will feel like a freaking genius!
- Tell yourself "I AM STRONG" you will feel invincible like Hercules!
- Tell yourself "I AM ENOUGH!" you will be enough!

- **YOU ARE WHAT YOU TELL YOURSELF YOU ARE! PLAIN AND SIMPLE!**

Change your thoughts and it will change your world! Watch what you think about yourself because YOU are listening! If you continuously put yourself down and berate yourself for every little thing you do wrong, then you will live in a world of "victim consciousness." I know this because I ruled this world by my own self-destructive measures! I was the Queen of the Castle in this negative world. It takes years of practice to catch a negative thought and change it into a positive one. As any other habit to change, it takes time, dedication and persistence.

Most times we are seeking fulfillment of ourselves for we are empty, and we look to external sources when the key lies deep within ourselves. We need only seek and we shall find. Can you differentiate between loneliness and solitude? Loneliness is when you are unhappy to be alone. Solitude is when you are happy and grateful to be alone. Which one are you? Just make sure your solitude isn't becoming an isolation craving to avoid/escape the world. There is a fine line that needs to be assessed from time to time. But if your time needed to recharge from the world and refocus on what it is that you need, then you just do whatever it is you need to do. Depending on the individual, time spent alone can be exciting or exhausting. Ask yourself this at different times when you think you are lonely. Personally, I need to recharge and focus on my inner strength and my time alone is very precious indeed! I cherish it and value it like no other. Instead of persistently dwelling on how alone you feel, move forward and do things to get your mind off what you are feeling. I have listed a few ideas to hopefully inspire you to move in the direction that feels right for you keeping in mind everyone is different and has various needs.

- First of all, identify the reasons why you feel lonely
- Start a journal and start tracking what you are feeling and when
- Seek professional counselling about your situation
- Recognize that you are NOT alone feeling this way
- Volunteer in your community; it is a wonderful way to get out of the house and meet other people.
- Meditate/contemplate; both work miracles in tuning yourself into your higher power; it clears your mind and brings awareness and understanding.
- Join a gym and take class like swimming; cycling; Zumba class; jogging or Yoga.
- Try outdoor skating or fishing; take a walk in the park or go on a picnic
- Learn a new skill (Art classes, cooking classes, sewing or other craft, etc.)
- Do social activities by yourself; don't let being alone stop you
- Keep yourself busy; don't sit at home dwelling on your misery
- Post sticky notes on your bathroom mirror or fridge with positive "I AM" statements about yourself and read them out loud every day.

These give you an idea of what things are out there for you to do. But it really boils down to you and only you. What is it you want out of life? Do you want to stay in your bubble of self-pity or do you want to take that scary first step and slowly start to change your ways? Only you can decide which direction you are willing to sail your ship. Take the time you need to write down what it is you really want in life; write goals and give yourself a timeline in order to accomplish them. Be kind to yourself if you need more time to achieve them. Don't beat yourself up over the little things as you are the one who decides what is on your plate. If it gets to be too much, simply remove an item and you will feel the stress leave your shoulders immediately! Works for me every single time!

Your beliefs become your thoughts,
Your thoughts become your words,
Your words become your actions,
Your actions become your habits,
Your habits become your values,
Your values become your destiny!

~Mahatma Ghandi~

STOP AND REFLECT

1. What do you tell yourself with the "I AM" factor? Be honest with yourself. Does it reflect a negative aspect? What can you do to change the negative connotations you put in that sentence?

_____

_____

_____

_____

2. Make a list of "I AM" sentences that reflect positive values you own. It's too easy to write negative ones. Read these positive sentences about yourself daily or just when you need a personal boost.

_____

_____

_____

_____

3. How can you engage in your own creativity when you start to feel lonely?

_____

_____

_____

_____

4. Does time spent alone keep you from living a happy, fulfilled life?

_____

_____

_____

_____

_____

5. Write down here some activities you can do to get yourself moving off the couch and into something else.

_____

_____

_____

_____

_____

Chapter 3:

MAYA - THE WORLD OF ILLUSION

ILLUSION:

Something that deceives by producing a false or misleading impression of reality. A thing that is or is likely to be wrongly perceived or interpreted by the senses; a deceptive appearance or impression; a false idea or belief.[4]

Some illusions are based on general assumptions the brain makes during perception. The term *illusion* refers to a specific form of sensory distortion. Unlike a hallucination, which is a distortion in the absence of a stimulus, an illusion describes a misinterpretation of a true sensation.

Illusions are all around us; they dominate our world everywhere we turn. Most of us however, have had their senses dulled by society and what the media wants us to believe. The world has become so twisted and upside down in putting up a curtain to hide the real truth, that we have in fact been wrapped up in a whirlwind of deception, false appearances and distortion of the truth. It gets to a point when nobody really knows what to believe! This is why it is crucial

---

4   www.dictionary.com/browse/illusion

to everyone reading this book that you discover *your own truth*! You have to pull aside the curtain of illusion and find out what is waiting on the other side. You have to learn to question everything you have ever been taught to be true. Who in fact says it is? A lot of the time, your parents teach you what their parents taught them, so on and so forth. Who says it is right? Ask your own questions and find your own answers; don't take for granted the fact that just because your parents say it's true that it really is. It is also very easy to be misled by illusions of our own creation. Sometimes it's easier to believe what we want to believe rather than deal with the reality of what is staring at us in the face. The great thing about creating our own illusions is as simple as this: you created it therefore you have the power to dissolve it!

I was so very naïve most of my life and spent it living an illusion, believing things to be true when in fact they were not. I could not recognize the difference between reality and illusion which played such an important role in my life. I was so wrapped up with what society was telling me how to look, act, dress and behave, that I was sidetracked from the truth. I had become a puppet of deception and sad to say, it took me until I was 40 and in recovery to discover the cold, hard truth that my entire life was a lie! Everything I thought to be true was in fact an illusion! How can this be? Where was I for the last 40 years? I had to put up an image of who I was and wear many different masks because I truly didn't know what was up or down; I didn't know who I was or who I was supposed to be. The main thing I had learned as a child was to keep secrets and not show the world what was really going on in my life. What goes on behind closed doors stays behind closed doors. Nobody would ever guess what horrors were really happening with the family that seemed to be perfect. Even the family pictures depicted perfection, which I despised because I knew the dark secrets of this family. Everything that ever happened to me was hiding deep inside me, and to the world, I looked beautiful and happy when I really wasn't. It was all a mass illusion that I didn't even realize I was creating for myself at the time. I so wanted someone to love me that I put on a mask that hid the emptiness deep inside; that giant bottomless hole with no end to its darkness. I became a chameleon; I would change and become the person others wanted me to be and at whatever price it cost me. The emptiness was so dark and deep that I would do almost anything for love. I had so many personas going such as playing the hero of the family, the caregiver, the party girl, the strong one, etc., that it took quite some time to unravel the many layers I had going on. A painful process indeed because the minute I thought I had it all figured out, WHAM! Another painful layer blindsided me out of nowhere. When would it ever end? Would I ever discover who I really was underneath all the processed BS that was my reality? Would I ever learn to love myself for *who* I was and not for what the world wanted me to be? I truly didn't know.

This world of illusion truly began to breed itself under the fine layer of my skin after the horrible incident with my foster family. I suddenly blossomed from an ugly duckling that I had been living the first 15 years of life, to a beautiful and graceful swan. The transformation was almost overnight it seemed and this brought me to a whole new level with my self-esteem and peers. I suddenly began to do local hair shows and fashion shows in both my hometown and the adjoining one as well. I took ballet and jazz dance lessons and started doing dance shows and became locally known. All of a sudden, I was on TV commercials and found myself in Montreal on a TV contest for modeling where I made it to the finals but didn't win. My local popularity skyrocketed and I even began talking to the local schools about my experiences on TV and as a model, and was also featured in the local newspaper. This was a big thing in my small town. I went from being a reject to being a star in no time! Now I had a goal; it was to pursue a career in modeling in Montreal once I turned 18. When that day finally came, I took some modeling classes and began the journey into the world of mass illusion.

I quickly realized how lonely and dark the journey would be for me. I was never good enough, thin enough or pretty enough. Nothing about me was right for the modeling world and this played a huge part in my allowing things to happen and not having a voice in my own story called life. I developed an eating disorder and would not eat; what I did eat was automatically thrown up right after as I just couldn't live with the guilt of not having personal discipline when it came to food. This was my secret and personal fight with myself. I was trying so hard to be perfect so someone could love me for what I looked like, so I portrayed an image of this skinny, well-dressed, and beautiful young woman. The modeling world lives by these unspoken rules and I truly believed them to be golden rules to live by. I felt I could only go so far in Montreal as a model because I didn't quite fit the mold being 5'8 and 125 lbs. I dropped down to 115lbs and was still considered too fat to be a model. This wreaked havoc on my mental state of mind. My self-esteem was already shot and this didn't help things at all because I still never felt good enough, thin enough or pretty enough. I truly believed I was under-standard and unworthy but I dreamed of modeling to be my path of life so I continued to work at it with all my heart. I had an image to uphold for my family as well and felt the unspoken pressure to succeed.

I was working as a waitress and had saved enough money to go to Miami for 6 months to better my modeling opportunities. I was alone and living in a world where I couldn't work as I didn't have a work visa, so was using my personal money and trying to make it last as long as possible. I was naïve to the ways of the Miami modeling world and soon was lured into a modeling session that turned ugly really quick. I accepted an invitation to go out with the photographer after the shoot so I could meet some people in the industry and hopefully gain employment. After having a diet 7-UP (alcohol was too fattening), I felt uncomfortable and wanted to leave, but he convinced me to stay for another soda. I accepted and was simply waiting for the opportunity to make my exit. Next thing I knew, I woke up naked with the man on top of me. I tried to get him off of me, but I couldn't move my body. It was as if my muscles refused to move and weighed 100 pounds each! How can this be and what in the world is happening to me? I felt as if I was out of my body watching what was going on down below unable to change the situation, feeling completely helpless. He was hurting me and laughing at it saying I wanted it. It seemed like time had stopped and eternity dwelled in that dark moment. When it was finally over, my body felt like an anchor. I was unable to say anything due to the grogginess of my mind and spirit. I struggled to get up and fought to understand what had just happened as I searched for my clothes, shame written all over me.

The many questions I had remained unanswered as I groggily made my way home, truly not understanding how in the world what just happened. I wasn't drunk as I was drinking pop, so how come I didn't remember anything? I would never in a million years sleep with a stranger so how did I end up in his bed? It was a complete memory blackout; one minute I was drinking a pop thinking of a way to get home, and the next minute I was being violated in a way I did not agree to. I just couldn't put the pieces together and never for once thought I had been drugged in order to be raped, then told it was my fault and that I wanted it the whole time. I was so disgusted and felt so completely dirty that I couldn't shower enough to rid myself of the filthy, slimy feeling I had all over me. I never told anyone of this experience due to my personal shame and believing it was completely my fault. I had so many unanswered questions and the only thing I could come up with was that I was really the one to blame. It was my fault; after all he did say I wanted it. How can that be? I did not agree to that at all! I was so ashamed and confused that I just wanted to disappear.

While I was in Miami, I did a few commercials, photo shoots and fashion shows, but the season was over and I ran out of money. I did meet another photographer who even though he looked at me with disdain because I was "too fat" at 115 lbs., he saw how good my pictures turned out and gave me a connection in New York City and told me to come there. This became my goal and I worked hard to get there. I decided I would try even harder to be perfect for this chance in New York that I finally had. Still feeling completely worthless, I went back to Montreal to work again serving in a bar to save money to get to my modelling goal in New York. I did a few more photo shoots while in Montreal, but was told again I didn't fit the modeling criteria and that I would never make it. I finally managed to save up enough money and get on the next bus there.

When I arrived, I went straight to the agency that had hired me; they already a room for me in an apartment with a film producer. I was to share the room with another model from Paris who was the picture perfect idea of what a model should me; very tall and very, very thin, with exotic looks and a perfect body. This didn't help my already low self-esteem and self-worth; if anything, it made it worse because now I believed I wasn't right in body, height and size and shape. My anorexia/bulimia plummeted into the deep recesses of the sewers, and it's as if I had no control over it because I was so desperate to be perfect and wanted. I felt I had absolutely no voice in anything that was going on deep within me, but I still kept up the illusion that everything was ok for my family; that I was living the modeling dream when in reality I wasn't. I was miserable and hurting badly but just couldn't get myself to tell the truth about it.

The loneliness was excruciating and I spent many a night in tears unable to talk about it. The one thing that did save me and gave me strength and hope to continue on, was singing the HU. I sang this word day and night, and it soothed my hurting heart as I struggled through the harsh world I was living in. This word when sung for 20 minutes a day brings inner peace and understanding; I didn't feel so alone when I contemplated on this. I would create spiritual exercises throughout my contemplation sessions where I could escape to a happier place. My dreams at night brought me to beautiful places and I met many incredible spiritual beings who shared their words of wisdom, which in turn helped me through the dark nights of Soul. There were so many little things that would happen to me during any random moment to show me that I wasn't completely alone, which strengthened my Faith. One example of this was the one day I absolutely needed to call the agency and had no money at all. It was crucial for me to call, but I was in an industrial area with no stores around. As I was walking down an unfamiliar street, I suddenly got a very clear vision of my index finger going into a slot of a telephone booth and finding a quarter. The vision disappeared as fast as I got it. My gut instinct told me to turn left at the next street so I did and continued to walk down to the next corner. I saw a telephone booth across the street and thought of my vision the minute earlier. I laughed and told myself there was no way that was possible, but decided to go check it out anyways as I had nothing to lose. I crossed the street and just like my vision, I put my index finger into the slot and low and behold if I didn't pull out a quarter! Unbelievable! I couldn't believe my eyes and as I laughed at the whole situation, my eyes drifted upwards the length of the phone and incredibly saw 2 words engraved: "THANK GOD!" How amazing was this situation? There was the quarter I needed to call the agency and I had the vision to show me where to find it in an area I had never been in. I thanked God over and over for this little gift. I had many of these "gifts" all the time during my stay in hectic New York City proving to me there was indeed a Higher Power that was continuously watching over me.

During the day, I would go all over downtown Manhattan to up to 15 auditions a day with on average 150 other models all striving for the same job. I constantly compared myself to others and felt beneath them all and worthless. I felt like I didn't meet up to their standards and didn't fit in. The way the other girls looked at me with disdain made me squirm in my seat and falter when it came time for the interview. One place wanted me for a cover of their magazine, but I would have to be topless with only jewelry; I just couldn't do it. She simply shrugged her shoulders and said it was ok because there were 200 girls right behind me who gladly would and shut the door in my face. I was a tad put off, but didn't care because at least I had stood up to my personal morals. I would not stoop to going naked just for a possible cover; besides during a photo shoot there is always at least 10-15 people in the room with you all looking at you. My incredible low self-esteem would not allow me to be topless in front of all those people anyway, so it really didn't matter to me. There was just no way

I would do it and stood firm on that point; that went for the whole idea of "sleeping my way to the top" like so many other girls I knew. I refused to do that either. I would rather quit modeling if it came to that; my experience in Miami still affected me greatly.

I needed 8 pages in magazines to be given a working visa in the US, and I only had 6 at the time; money was running out really quickly for me. Although I truly loved New York and the whole modeling experience, I felt it was my time to leave and head back to Montreal. The agency wanted to "loan" me $5,000 so I could continue to get my last 2 needed pages in magazines for my work visa, but my gut instincts wouldn't allow me to do that. I may have been naïve in many areas, but the idea of owing $5,000 to people I really didn't know in NYC on top of all places wasn't sounding like a great idea to me. I could easily be made to "pay off the debt" in some other way and I wasn't going down that road. Something was changing in me, and the constant rejection and cruelty of the people in the industry was too much for my gentle nature. I just didn't have the backbone and aggressive personality for the sharks treading in the water all around me. I started to see through the mask of illusion, the cold hard facts of what was beneath the façade of the industry. This constant feeling of not measuring up and being the underdog was finally getting to me. Right before I was to make a final decision on where I was going to end up, I went to visit my friend Alain in Washington, DC for a month. There was a Spiritual seminar going on there that I wanted to attend, so this was a golden opportunity for me to figure things out on the deeper, inner side of things.

After the seminar, I went to an old, beautiful church that had the most incredible gardens surrounding it. I decided to go sit on a bench and contemplate my life and the choices I had. After sitting there for a while, I went back to my friend's place and had an afternoon nap. I instantly fell into a dream where I had returned to this beautiful garden at the old church and was sitting on that very same bench. A figure approached me; he had long white, flowing hair and beard to go with it. He wore a long white tunic that reminded me of a monk-type being. The love and kindness flowing from him were incredible and so soothing to my troubled Soul. He sat beside me and spoke softly about the upcoming decisions in my life.

He said I had two choices. The first choice would be to go to Ecuador with my friend and have a good and happy remainder of this lifetime. The second would be to go back to Montreal and face the "Eye of the Hurricane," in which I would encounter many hardships, and chances were that I would most likely not survive it. But if I did, the rewards would be endless. He continued to say that either choice would be ok, but that at some point I would need to repay off a karmic debt; there was no escaping that fact. It was entirely my choice as to when I wanted to deal with it; either this lifetime or the next one. I sat there thinking what kind of choice is that? Geez! That's really not a fair choice at all! As he sat there quietly awaiting my response, I could feel the love flowing from him like I had never experienced before. I thought to myself: "Who could have that much love to give? It is so very beautiful and uplifting!" As I sat there quietly contemplating my decision, I already knew in my heart what the choice would be. I would have to go back to Montreal and face the "Eye of the Hurricane" in this lifetime and deal with the karma that was due unto me. I looked into the deep depths of his wise eyes and sadly told him my decision. He looked at me with complete compassion then nodded his head with understanding. His parting words upon my awakening were, "I will always be with you if you need me; you just have to ask." I awoke with such a feeling of dread that I cried. I continued to cry all the way home on the train back to Montreal, terrified of my decision, but knowing it was the right thing to do. The pain awaiting me once I got there would be most definitely life altering for sure.

When it comes to illusions, I am not talking about hallucinations; they are 2 distinct things. The illusion I am referring to is that of what you *think* is happening and the reality of *what* is happening. Hallucinations are sensations that appear real but are created by your mind. I spent my entire life living in the illusion that being socially accepted for your looks and size is what is important in life. This is a *huge* illusion that society throws at us and most of us fall for it! I most certainly did for most of my life. It was because I felt I did not meet up to society's ridiculous expectations, I felt unworthy and didn't feel up to par with everyone else. This is so very false! This is the sort of thing that I am talking about. It is like those in your life that smile to your face and tell you one thing, then turn around behind your back and slander you like no tomorrow. The illusion is that you truly believe they are honest and true to you, but they really aren't. You have to learn to decipher the illusion when it knocks on your door. How does one do that? Sadly, sometimes it takes life's harsh experiences to recognize it when it comes.

Recognition of it can also come in the form of intuition. If your instinct is telling you that something isn't right; follow it! Your gut instinct will always guide you to where you need to be, so learn to tune in to it and listen to what it is telling you. We have all had moments where your instinct was screaming at you to do something and you didn't listen and proceeded to do your own thing, with the result being you saying:" OH! Why didn't I listen to that feeling I had earlier!" Now it's too late and you have to follow through with the consequences of your actions. Note to self: "Next time...follow your gut feeling!" These gut feelings will help you navigate many of the illusions this world throws at us daily!

Be mindful of what is going on around you. Watch with a close eye to the actions and behaviours of those closest to you. If they are negative in any way, shape or form, ask yourself this: "Do I really want to become like these people around me? Is it really that important to fit in with a crowd of people who will mock, laugh at and undermine the hurting?" Really evaluate who is in your crowd and what *illusion* they are throwing out there? Ask yourself why is it so important to feel accepted by them? What is going on with *you* that you feel the need to be accepted?

Illusions come in many forms so be aware of your surroundings and pay close attention to what is really going on around you. Learn to have the "eyes to see" and the "ears to hear" what is *really* going on within yourself so you will be better prepared to face the illusions of the world! They are all around us integrating us with false images and false pretenses. Once you learn to decipher the masks of illusion, you will gain a sudden clarity of mind that will give you an advantage over life in general. You will be able to read through the falseness of people that are trying to *lure* you into something you don't necessarily want or need in your life. Taking the time to learn to *read* people will give you and edge and may ultimately save you from a bad or unwanted situation. Sadly, there are many people out there with very bad intentions who will fill you with lies and false truths, so be very aware and take your time before you jump into anything new with someone. Do your own research; be your own detective and find out a few things beforehand as it may just save you a lot of grief down the road...

I like the idea that we build up these walls or rules or laws to maintain our reality, and when they fall away, you're left with a whole bunch of illusions. Smoke and mirrors.

~Sarah McLachlan~

STOP AND REFLECT:

1. What is going on in your life that you feel is pulling a curtain over your eyes?

   _____

   _____

   _____

   _____

   _____

   _____

2. What can you do to pull away the curtain of illusion surrounding you? Whom do you surround yourself with? Are they toxic in getting you to believe in something that is not true? Are they feeding you illusions and if so, why are you choosing to believe them?

   _____

   _____

   _____

   _____

   _____

   _____

3. If you really think about it, what is it in your life you feel is just an illusion? Is it a person, place or thing, the social front that we live in? Illusion of happiness?

_____

_____

_____

_____

_____

_____

4. When it comes to illusions, there is a fine line that we need to cross and be able to recognize when it comes our way. What tool can you use to help you see through this? Meditation? Contemplation? Tuning into your inner senses? Writing? Paying attention to the subtle signs?

_____

_____

_____

_____

_____

_____

5. What experiences have you had in the past that have now helped you see things in a different light to navigate your life today?

_____

_____

_____

_____

_____

_____

_____

_____

_____

_____

_____

_____

_____

_____

_____

_____

_____

_____

Chapter 4

EYE OF THE HURRICANE

DESPAIR:

Loss of hope; hopelessness, to lose, give up, or be without hope. Desperation, despondency refer to a state of mind caused by circumstances that seem too much to cope with. Despair suggests total loss of hope, usually accompanied by apathy and low spirits: *He sank into despair after the bankruptcy.* Desperation is a state in which loss of hope drives a person to struggle against circumstances, with utter disregard of consequences: *In desperation, they knocked down the door.* Despondency is a state of deep gloom due to loss of hope and a sense of futility and resignation: *despondency after a serious illness.*[5]

Despair is a deep state of mental apathy that can lead to acts of extreme desperation even to suicide attempts. Despair is a state that many people in the world today have faced in the past or are currently facing. Circumstances seem to pile up against the individual and all hope is lost. The strength to carry on seems to melt away in the desert sun. Where do you get the courage to get back up on your feet and try again? Our choices in life may have been not the best at times, and now suddenly we are faced with seemingly insurmountable problems.

5   http://www.dictionary.com/browse/despair

How do we face them alone? How do we keep up the image that everything is alright when really nothing is farther from the truth! The hardest part about it is being honest with oneself, acknowledging the fact that maybe it is our own fault somewhere down the line that we find ourselves in these difficult circumstances. Taking responsibility for our actions and thus the consequences is not an easy thing to accept. Many times, however, circumstances are beyond our control such as illness. Illness will rock your world inside out, upside down, then all around for some more shaking far beyond what the eye can see. People lose everything they have due to illness and even become homeless as they have no way of paying their bills. How much more desperate can you get than that? I have seen it happen many times throughout the years. Where do you find the will to get back up and start all over again when circumstances are working against you? How do you find Hope in Hopelessness? Where do you find the sun in a rainstorm of hardships? How do you see the positive in such a negative situation where troubles keep on hitting you from all sides? How do you keep the Faith that there is a God or Higher Power out there who is watching over you throughout these difficult times? If there is a God, why in the world isn't HE doing anything about it? How can a loving God stand there and let all these horrible things happen? These are all questions I asked myself throughout most of my life as I spent a good deal of my life living in a desperate situation, struggling just to survive every single day.

When I stepped off that train coming in from Washington, all hell broke loose. It was as if the hurricane had arrived and was patiently waiting for me to get there. Unsuspectingly, I walked right into its wide open arms, where it embraced me like a fly trapped in a spider web.

I had found a summer job working at a Hotel where there was a pool and bar on the roof. The last night of work for the season, I left with $700 cash in my wallet that I had made in tips; it was for my rent and groceries. After closing and having our end of season party, we all headed down to the famous Dunn's for Montreal Smoked Meat sandwiches. We ate, laughed and had a great time, then I got into a cab at 3AM and headed home. I paid the cab and crossed the sidewalk to get to my apartment. I lived on a street that had very poor lighting and absolutely no traffic. I had on a one piece spandex legging outfit with a giant t-shirt from work that covered everything to my mid thighs, and was carrying a backpack with all my personal belongings, wallet and house keys. As I fumbled with my backpack looking for my house keys, I noticed 4 guys coming down the sidewalk close to me, but didn't pay any attention as I was trying to get my keys and couldn't see anything as it was so dark.

Next thing I know, I felt a sharp pain in my head and was being dragged around the corner to the alley where they proceeded to attempt to rip off my clothes. Words cannot describe the fear that raced through my blood as I knew full well what was coming. Thankfully, I lost consciousness for the time being. I woke up with a man on top of me violating me painfully, and attempted to get him off of me but to no avail. "Stop it" and "Get off of me" had absolutely no effect on him whatsoever; if anything, it urged him on more. The ultimate power he must have been experiencing overtook his sense of right or wrong and he was thriving on the wrong side of it at my expense. I couldn't seem to move or even gather up the strength to fight him off. When he finally got off of me, I was able to wobbly get up and find some of my torn clothes. I was in an apartment and asked him how I got there as to my last recollection, I was in the alley being violated by 4 guys. He told me that he and his roommate came along and found me passed out on the ground, and that they had scared off the other guys. They brought me to their apartment and decided to have some fun. They both had a turn on me before the roommate left for work. This man who was in his forties at least, had decided to stay for some more action. My clothes were torn, my t-shirt wasn't anywhere to be found, my purse was gone with all the money I had for rent, and my wallet with all my ID, my house keys...everything was gone! My head hurt where I had been hit, my thoughts were all mixed up with random images of nastiness, and I was really confused as to what to do. I just couldn't seem to think straight and man...did I ever have a headache! How in the world was I supposed to get back in my own home? I asked him where I was and he said right beside your apartment...he was my neighbor! I was horrified! How could a neighbor do such a thing? How disgusting is that? I just couldn't believe it and needed to get out of there as fast as I could so I stumbled down the stairs to the store across the street to call the landlord. Not once did it occur to me that I should call the police. Why I didn't call them, I will never know. My main concern was to have a hot shower and try to wash the filth away as soon as I could. Maybe deep down inside I felt responsible for what just happened to me once again.

My landlord with whom I had a sometimes "friends with benefits" relationship came to deliver the keys and when I told him what had happened, he flew into a fit of rage and grabbed a baseball bat I had by the door in case of intruders, and took off running towards the neighbor's house. He pounded the door and walls screaming like a madman for them to come out and get what they deserved for doing what they did to me. After what seemed like forever he came back in to find me in a state of distress crying uncontrollably. He came to console me and asked me what happened so I told him the whole story. He was disgusted and said he was so sorry that I had to go through that. As he held me, he became aroused and started to kiss me gently at first, then with more force. I pushed him away in disgust as the last thing on my mind was having sex after what I had just been through, but he brought me back into his arms and held me there telling me he would just hold me. Before I knew it, he had me pinned underneath him and pulled my pants down because he insisted that he be the one to remove all fear of sex within me! Can you believe that? He kept telling me that it was like riding a horse and if you fall, the trick to kill the fear of it is to get back up and do it again. He said that he should be the one to help me "get back on the horse" otherwise I would never be the same again. He enjoyed our encounters and didn't want to lose that so he would help me deal with it. I began to cry with horror at what he was implying and I said," NO! Get off of me!" He flat out refused and violently thrust himself into me so that I would not become "frigid" as so many women who have been raped do. He held my arms pinned above my head so I couldn't fight him. He was rambling on about cold women and he didn't want me to become one. He was insistent that he was only showing me his love and concern for my mental health. He was certain he was doing me a favor and helping me out, and in the long run, I would thank him for it one day! Unbelievable! He was incredibly rough and he hurt me even worse than the neighbor did. I kept telling him to get off of me but he kept repeating that he was doing me a favor. I just couldn't fight back anymore; I had absolutely no strength and my headache was intense with throbbing waves of nausea coursing through my body. It seemed to go on forever until finally it was over and he, feeling he had just done the world of men a favor, left. The complete betrayal I felt ran deep and I was in complete shock. I could barely walk, was hurting all over my body, so I stumbled and half-crawled my way to the shower where I remained for 3 hours. I couldn't move and the numbness I felt ran deep. There is not enough soap and water in the world that could remove the filth that was covering my entire body and Soul! It was engrained to the very core of my being, or so it felt. The rest of that night was spent on the floor by the shower curled into a ball crying my eyes out. Every part of my body, mind and Soul hurt deeply. The dark hole of loneliness and despair had no words, only never-ending tears. Talk about having a "Dark night of Soul"...I didn't feel as if I had anyone to talk to about it so I didn't. My immediate family was too absorbed in their own struggles to have me make it worse with this story, so I just kept it to myself. No one ever knew.

Even my very good friend Denis, who had supported me in every way a friend could over the years, was unable to help me. Denis had been with me since the very beginning of my arrival in Montreal and knew me like no other, but even his friendship and all the great and goofy times we shared couldn't help me. I had crossed over to a dark place where only deep counselling would be able to put a spark of light back into my eyes...I had to learn the very hard lesson that help would come to me if only I would take the necessary steps to go find the proper counselling to get through it. Sadly, it would take a few years for me to learn that lesson. Instead, I chose to pretend it never happened. What I didn't realize that by doing just that, I was actually letting it stew in its own force and gather strength to grow into an inner demon that would chase me later in life. It was to grow so big that conquering this incredible force of nature would prove to be quite the challenge.

I quickly came to realize that I had a serious problem on my hands that needed to be addressed soon. How could I possibly continue to live in that apartment with the landlord coming and going as he pleased in my space, and especially after what he did to me? He didn't see anything wrong with what he did, and he would continue to come and do it again and again. I felt as if I would never have a voice in the situation and I needed to get out of there as soon as possible. A few days after this all occurred, with my head still hurting, I finally had no choice but to leave the apartment to go try to look for work as the world does go on and I did need money to find another place to live. As I stood at the bus stop on the corner, I saw the neighbor who raped me across the street standing there just looking at me and smiling a sick smile. I froze with fear and was completely paralyzed into inaction. I couldn't breathe or think of what to do next. What if he came over and started talking to me? What would I say? How could I handle it? I was terrified of the sick look on his face telling me he was re-living his enjoyment of the other night as he recognized me from afar. Who would stop him from trying to do it again? I knew right then I could no longer live there and needed to leave... NOW! This realization completely threw me off as I had no money and nowhere to go. I had no more job as the hotel was just a summer thing, so what was I going to do? I was completely overwhelmed with what to do next and I had absolutely no help from anyone; I was completely alone. My brain was so full of hurt and confusion that the thought of even looking for a job was overwhelming to me, so I ambled around Montreal lost in a fog of my own dark thoughts. I ended up in a liquor store and spent the very last of my money on a giant bottle of wine, thinking I would go sit in a park somewhere to think about my situation and a possible solution to it. I am not sure exactly how it happened, but I ended up on the biggest bridge in

Montreal, Le Pont Jacques-Cartier, where many a sad Soul had taken their final leap in life. The more I drank the wine, the more my pain was being released from the inner depths of my Soul.

I sat and watched the busy nightlife of the beautiful city I loved so much, and thought how could I feel so alone amidst one million people? I had absolutely no one to talk to about what had happened and what I was going through now. I simply wanted some help and guidance, and even God wasn't returning my calls of pain. My prayers and tears seemed to be lost in the howling wind and the darkness of the night. The wine had taken its toll on my thought process, and I could no longer see anything but the darkness within. I stood on the side of the bridge railing looking over it to the deep swirling waters of the St. Lawrence River below. It seemed to hypnotize me and I felt as if it were calling me to jump in. It was a cold, dark night and the winds were howling as if to express their anger at the world resonating my exact feelings. I cried to God above; "Why have you forsaken me?" How could you let this happen? I am a good person and would never hurt anyone...where are you? How could you leave me alone? I HATE YOU!" I screamed over and over and cried from the depths of my Soul as the pain through my ragged and bruised body. So very alone in my misery and not necessarily wanting to die, just wanting the pain to stop and have loving arms hold me to tell me it would be alright.

I didn't have any of that, and just couldn't seem to see any light at the end of the tunnel, so I put a leg over the rail and was seemingly transfixed by the dark waters below that were taunting me to come. As I stood there ready to take the final leap in life, I sensed a presence coming at me from the left. It was a man with long golden hair and blue eyes. He wore thin rimmed glasses but the look of love in his eyes was unmistakable. He walked slowly holding a bicycle and he approached me with a Spiritual Grace I had only seen in my dreams. The aura around him made me trust him immediately as he leaned the bike to the side and came to put his arm around me to pull me off the railing of the bridge. He very gently sat me down beside him and kept his arm around me never saying a single word. He sensed my deep pain so just continued to hold me as I cried and cried my tears of deep despair. We sat there like that, until at one point I made a run for the railing again as the pain ripped through me, but once again he simply put his arm around me and sat me back down. When my sobs finally subsided, he pulled me to my feet, took my hand and walked me off the bridge. A taxi suddenly appeared out of nowhere with both of us getting in, and I was taken to a hospital where I could get the help I needed. I mumbled a thank you and never saw him again.

I didn't stay there very long because the doctor was crazier than I could have ever imagined. He flat out terrified me as I sat there listening to him ramble on about how he was in control and would decide my fate in life; I knew right then and there he would drug me heavily, lock me up and then God only knows what other horrors awaited me. I could see the madness in his eyes as he looked me over head to toe...Yikes! If I didn't get out of there soon, this could very well be the end of the road for me. I went along with his little game and agreed with what he was saying so as not to tip him off, but managed to escape that nightmarish place the very next day. There was no way on earth I would stay there with that fanatical doctor to do whatever he pleased at my expense! I don't think so buddy! I may be depressed but I am not crazy!

I managed to go to Social Services and get some assistance from them with a place to stay and some money, but the pain in my burdened heart was nowhere close to being fixed. It was only a matter of time before the nights became a traumatic time of reliving what had happened and my feeling it was my fault. My self-worth plummeted as I realized I would no longer ever go back to being a model as I felt not good enough for anything in life. What was I going to do? The depression I felt was so dark and so deep that I truly felt as if I had nothing to live for. All I wanted was love and happiness, yet I lived in a world of darkness and despair. I did attend a rape clinic for some counselling, but the thought of going to the police with a story I truly believed was entirely my fault, which I now know it wasn't, didn't appeal to me. The counsellor kept pushing it so I never went back. Boy! Was I ever wrong about that one! I should've gone and had those men prosecuted for the crime they did against me. I didn't have the fight against what I thought would be classified as my fault or "consensual sex" when it wasn't that way at all. The mere thought of facing angry men filled me with a fear that ran so deep it paralyzed me to the very core of my being. I just couldn't do it. To this day, not a single person who has ever abused me, whether it be sexual or physical was ever charged with the violation done unto me. How many women out there have the same situation? Raped and beaten, but nothing is done about it whether it be by the justice system or the women themselves out of fear and guilt. Many women suffer in silence just like I did, and my hopes for this book is for those hurting to find the courage to speak out about their story of abuse. Many women carry around the burden as if it was their fault, when in reality, no-one has the right to violate your body in any way, shape or form. I hope to raise awareness on this matter.

I tried talking to my family, but they were too busy with their own struggles and I didn't want to burden them more. My solution was to swallow a whole bottle of pills and as I lay there waiting for them to take effect, I called my mother and told her what I had done as a last ditch effort to get help. She managed to convince me to go get the kind, old gentleman who was my neighbor to bring me to the hospital. He did just that and my stomach was quickly pumped with charcoal in the Emergency Room. This was by far the most painful and humiliating experience I had ever had with regards to the physical state. I was left in the busy emergency hall for everyone to see me excrete and vomit everything that I had so dangerously ingested. The nurses were too busy to come help me or clean me up and the humiliation ran deep. There was a woman who was dying in the room right beside where I was lying, and her family kept going by me as they walked in and out of her room. I laid there so ashamed of myself, horrified by my state of appearance. Talk about a lesson in humility...

The mother of the dying woman came over to me and sat with me. With loving hands she washed my face and gave me ice chips to soothe my thirst. With tears in her eyes, she asked me why I would try to take away something that is so precious such as life. She couldn't do anything for her dying daughter in the other room, so she transferred her love that was sorely needed to a hurting Soul like me. She tenderly and lovingly washed me up in order to give me some dignity back. We both cried and seemingly the harder I cried, the more love she gave me. It was a transfer of love in the purest form and given so freely! We talked a bit about my life but I was so ashamed of my actions and predicament that it was difficult for me to find words. Instead I dwelled in the love she gave to me like a starving child. I was so very grateful for her loving attention and thanked her in saying that she had just freely given to me the very thing I was looking for: love. I soaked up the love she so freely gave to me like a sponge in water. That in itself was the healing power I needed to start getting back to thinking straight again. All I needed was love and she gave me just that...all that she had to give. In that moment, she gave me the love I had been searching for.

With that my own family arrived to see me. They had travelled 6 hours from my hometown and were rightfully worried about me. I could clearly see from my bed that they had their own issues and were all wrapped up in their own pain; I had just taken mine a step further. It was pointless for me to even begin to talk about what really was going on so I kept it superficial and never once mentioned anything that had happened to me since Miami. In my eyes, it was all my fault and I was to blame so why burden them with it when it was clear to me they were fighting their own battles. I turned my head to see the woman who had so lovingly taken care of me and wished I could have that. However, I understood that my own family was hurting just as bad as I was; the difference being they handled it differently. As I looked from their family to mine, I recognized that I had no place here; no help and I was on my own. I made the decision right there that as soon as I was released, I would have to go find my own help somewhere far from the darkness of Montreal. If I was going to get better whatsoever, I had to take a step somewhere I could find strength again and I chose that to be as far away as my welfare check would allow me...Jasper, Alberta.

Pain and despair can overcome almost any human being when the circumstances allow it. I was so young and so very alone with my pain. I had no one to guide me or show me how to help myself; it was me against the big, bad world and I felt I was losing the battle. What changed my perception on the matter was that woman who washed my face ever so lovingly. Somehow, somewhere deep down inside, her love touched me like no other. That flow of love as she ever so gently washed my face, gave me the strength to persevere no matter how alone I may have felt. It was as if her love recharged my batteries enabling me to continue to strive forward. The transfer of the love from a grieving mother over her dying daughter given to me so willingly and completely, was sheer healing unto my damaged Soul. The dozen of white roses I gave to her when I left, which my family had brought to me, was nothing in comparison to what had transpired between the two of us. I am not entirely sure if she realized just how profound her love touched me in a way that began a chain reaction of the healing process that I so desperately needed. Love truly is healing when given as well as it being received. Love is the cure for all life I believe. Love is all powerful and can bring damaged cells back to life.

How does one work through these difficult times you may ask yourself? The answer to that is: with great difficulty and much prayer for a better tomorrow. Even at that young age, I knew my environment wasn't healthy for me, so I took the steps necessary to make the changes I needed in order to pull through this. For me the solution was to move to the mountains of Jasper, Alberta, Canada. Every time I saw the mountains on TV, my breath would be taken away by their majesty. I knew it would be the perfect place to start over my life and get the healing I so desperately needed. I knew that I had to meet life halfway if I wanted to survive the darkness surrounding my every thought.

Whatever problems you may be facing right now can be overcome. Today I know this to be true. What I have learned is that the solution will not come find you as you lay on the couch motionless from all the pain and desperation. You have to somehow and someway find the strength to reach out and take that scary first step into the unknown. No matter if you cry the whole way there...be brave, take that first step and the Universe will conspire to assist you in some way via a source you may not have thought of. The Universe has a way of helping those who help themselves; the key is to have the eyes to see and the ears to hear what the Universe is trying to tell you. Every person you meet, every situation that comes your way, every choice you make is all part of a Divine Plan. Life is like unlocking a puzzle where you constantly try one piece over and over to find it doesn't belong anywhere, so you try another piece, and so on and so forth until finally after what seems like ages, it fits into another piece of the puzzle. You sigh with relief and feel good about this accomplishment, but cannot believe just how long it took you to find that one little piece. As your eyes wander over the 950 other pieces laying all over in one giant mess, you think to yourself: "WOW! Look at all the work I still have left...how discouraging is that?" Most people don't have the patience to sit there and finish it, or they get so frustrated and abandon the project. Most often what happens is that they become focused on all the pieces they have left to put together, instead of what they have already accomplished. Their focus is on the wrong pile and this easily can overwhelm them. Persistence is what pays off in the long run; especially in life. When one piece doesn't fit into the puzzle of life, you have to keep trying something different until the right piece comes along. Life is a game of patience, persistence and strategy one piece at a time, one step at a time. You have to look back when you are having a bad day and see just how far you have already come through trials and tribulations. If today is a bad day, acknowledge that and start over tomorrow. There's always another day to try again and again and again if need be. Just like looking for that one piece of the puzzle, keep trying until the right one comes along.

Life is hard, and for some reason it seems to be getting even harder to live in these times. Sometimes it can seem as if we are getting hit from all sides and don't know where to put our next footstep. Despair and depression can set in without you even realizing it and before you know it, you find yourself in a situation where only darkness exists. How do you help yourself? What do you do? Where do you go? My answer to that is that only you can figure out what you need in this life. I had to learn this the hard way. Nobody likes to hear that, but it's true. No-one can save you but yourself. You have to put in the effort; pick up the phone to find the help you need; go to counselling; take a class; find the necessary resources; cry the tears; feel the frustration and do whatever it takes to help yourself get to a better place in life. I understand the difficulty in trying to do that when you live amidst the darkness of pain and hardships, but ultimately you must ask yourself: "How badly do I want change? This is my current situation and I don't like it, so what can I do to help myself change it?" I can say from my own experience that the end result is worth every tear I shed. The complete transformation of my life was worth every single Kleenex I threw out.

At any given moment in time, you have the power to say" This is NOT how my story is going to end!" I truly believe that one of the reasons I survived, was because the fire inside of me burned brighter than any fire around me! If there is a spark left inside you, light it into a flame; nurture that flame to burn so bright you need sunglasses. Only *you* have the capability to do it for yourself! Like Ghandi says, "Be the change you wish see in the world"

"When our days become dreary with low-hovering clouds of despair, and when our nights become darker than a than a thousand midnights, let us remember that there is a creative force in the universe, working to pull down the gigantic mountains of evil, a power that is able to make a way of out of no way and transform dark yesterdays into bright tomorrows"

~Martin Luther King JR~ A Testament of Hope

STOP AND REFLECT:

1. Think of a time when you may have been going through a difficult time. What were your deepest, darkest thoughts? Answer with all your honesty.

_____

_____

_____

_____

2. How did you manage to pull yourself out of that negative, dark place?

_____

_____

_____

_____

3. If you or someone you know are currently experiencing these feelings, what can you do in order to get to a better place mentally? What resources are in your area that could assist?

_____

_____

_____

_____

4. Pain and despair can drain a person into not having the energy or motivation to move in the direction they need to go. Think about what baby steps you could take for yourself if you are currently experiencing this.

_____

_____

_____

_____

_____

5. Finding someone to talk to is crucial when it comes to internal pain, otherwise the pain will fester and rot inside thus creating a vortex of darkness that can suck you in deeper. Who is in your area that you could take a tentative step with in sharing what you are currently going through? Is there crisis line you can access? Can you write a letter to yourself then destroy it? Getting it out is crucial to your mental health. The letter can be as simple as saying: "I am hurting, someone please help me! I can't do this alone!"

_____

_____

_____

_____

_____

_____

Chapter 4: EYE OF THE HURRICANE

Chapter 5:

OUT OF THE DEPTHS OF DARKNESS

HOPE:

Hope is an optimistic attitude of mind that is based on an expectation of positive outcomes related to events and circumstances in one's life or the world at large. As a verb, its definitions include: "expect with confidence" and "to cherish a desire with anticipation".[6]

Hope will empower you to move despite circumstances that may seem out of your control. It will get you moving out of the situation that you may find yourself in and even give you the strength to fight your way out of the hole, into the warmth of the sun above. Hope can get the blood in your veins flowing again; it will make the sun shine brighter and warmer; it will make you hear the birds sing again and smell the flowers on the way; it will motivate you to accomplish anything you set your mind to! Hope can bring out the best in you and give you wings to fly high above any problems that you may be

---

6   https://en.wikipedia.org/wiki/Hope

facing. Hope will get you to put one foot in front of the other and get you walking that narrow path again.

Hope is by far the one thing that has saved me throughout all my trials and tribulations in life. It motivated me to get moving again regardless of all my inner turmoil. The love that lady from the Emergency Room passed on to me was powerful and pure enough to recharge my drained battery. Somehow, she had given me a gift far better than I could have ever imagined! She gave me HOPE! That one random act of love had planted a seed that things could somehow get better. Hope had suddenly shown its face deep inside my scarred Soul and gave me the motivation I needed to get up and move. The move I had decided upon was to go find healing in the mountains, as Montreal had absolutely nothing for me but darkness and nightmares. The beauty I used to see in this amazing city was now gone. Replacing it was a dark layer of filth that I felt just couldn't be washed off. I saw only desire in the eyes of men that looked at me when I walked down the street. I was terrified of even passing beside a stranger on the sidewalk for fear of being attacked. Fear ruled my world everywhere I went, especially in the subway systems and their pathways. I felt like I was prey in the eyes of all the men I encountered on the streets that looked at me. The deep rooted fear of being attacked again sent me into panic attacks and off to a dark place in my head I was so desperately trying to escape. Getting out of Montreal was my best solution and the healing power of the mountains was calling me very loudly. I followed my heart without second thought.

Once I was released from the hospital, I immediately hopped on the first train out of there with a one-way ticket to Jasper – as far as my money would allow me. I had $150.00 in my pocket and a big, ugly, old brown leather suitcase. I was off on a new adventure that I was certain would be far better than what I was leaving behind. As the train pulled out of the Montreal Station, the feeling of sheer relief I felt was powerful enough to make my knees weak and body shake with anticipation of a new beginning. I was on a new journey of self-discovery that I was sure would help me get out of the current messy situation I had found myself in. I had complete faith and hope that I could start fresh and give myself a second chance because certainly, no one else would do it for me.

Crossing Canada was an adventure in itself and I was filled with hope and truly felt I was making a healthy choice for myself that would help me heal and get better. No one seemed to be able to help me in Montreal and it was a dead end, so I had decided to create my own luck. Once the train pulled out of Edmonton and made its way past Hinton into the rolling hills of the Rocky Mountains, I felt the sheer thrill of excitement race through my veins. I just couldn't believe what my eyes were seeing for the very first time! I actually rubbed my eyes and pinched myself to see if I was dreaming! I could hardly believe that this incredibly breathtaking scenery was here in Canada! I was sitting in the upper car of the train where it has a dome of windows for viewing the sky and the majestic mountains. Their beauty took my breath away and I decided right then and there that no way I was ever going back to the craziness of the Montreal lifestyle. What those mountains did for me in those first few minutes of adjusting my brain to what it was I was looking at, had accomplished more healing than anything else in my entire lifetime!(besides the love of that mother of course) I was in complete and utter awe, sitting speechless as I dwelled in their silent majesty. The intense beauty and magnitude of the mountains moved something deep inside me and lifted me up to almost to the heavens above. I truly felt as if I was in heaven on earth, and I thanked God for putting the inspiration in my heart and showing me the way here. When I stepped off of that train and looked at my new surroundings, I was uplifted and certain I had made the right decision. I was grateful to be there as it was a new beginning for me and I felt hope and anticipation of a new life far, far away from my old nightmares. Here I was naively certain that nothing could hurt me. I was safe. I was given a second chance at life and I had decided to make it a good one. I immediately got a job housekeeping where they provided you a place to live with a roommate. At least it was something, even though I hated every minute of it...but who was I to complain as it was an income at least? Soon after that nasty work experience, I was able to move to a job at Marmot Basin working in the kitchen cafeteria, which gave me free skiing so life was good for the winter months. Besides, it gave me a chance to meet new and exciting people who were alive in their hopes and dreams, unlike the deadbeats that I had surrounded myself with in Montreal.

After some time spent in Jasper, I knew I needed something more than just a ski-bum life. I was falling into the negative crowd and drinking became an almost daily thing with these so called "friends". One dark night after the end of the ski season, I had run out of money and couldn't find a job so went to drink with friends to feel better, which was my first mistake. I blacked out and don't remember what happened, but I woke up in the hospital with my wrists having 28 stitches. Apparently, I had cut both wrists in a depressive, drunken state; I still was being held captive from the recurring nightmare of Montreal because I had never dealt with the trauma and pain. I had chosen to bury it and it came to show its ugly face when I wasn't expecting it. It was in the hospital that I spoke with a pastor and told him what had happened to me in Montreal, and that I was just trying to start my life over again. It was him who finally was able to connect me with Social Services and get me into school in Hinton to finish my grade 12 as well as some much needed counselling. Without him helping me, I would have had nothing and I believe he was put on my path for a reason. I am truly grateful for his assistance in my journey.

I had a powerful experience right after I left the hospital that changed everything for me. One night soon after my hospital release, I woke up at 3 AM sitting straight up in bed and saw a figure standing in the corner of the kitchen. It had a dark cloak and hood and stood at least 6 and a half feet high. It was just looking at me, so I thought to myself that a Guardian Angel must be watching over me because of what just happened. I went back to sleep and when I awoke a little later, the figure was gone. The next week, I awoke at 3 AM again to see the same figure standing there watching me, only this time it was standing by a post halfway the distance to my bed. It just stood there watching me, and this began to creep me out somewhat, so I kept looking to see if it was moving and thought, "OH! OK! It is still making sure I am alright!" The third week comes along, and I awoke again at around 3 AM to see the same cloaked dark figure, this time standing at the foot of my bed motioning to me. By now, it was so close that I could clearly see it was the Angel of Death coming for me as I had played with the fine cord that attaches us to life! I had misused it three times in a short period of time and he was letting me know that he was coming for me! I was sitting in bed wide awake clearly staring at the Angel of Death at my bedside beckoning me! Holy Crap! I did the only thing I could that had always helped me in past when dealing with scary situations...I sang HU. HU, this ancient name for God, is a love song to God. You sing it. And in singing it or holding it in your mind during times of need, it becomes a prayer. It becomes a prayer of the highest sort. Well, in this instant, I needed all the help I could get, especially from the one who holds all power: Almighty God! I sang the HU loud and strong while keeping my eyes on it just in case it moved towards me. Something completely unbelievable happened in the next instant that can only happen in movies, or so I thought. As I sang HU, the figure broke into a billion small particles and fell into a heap of dust on the floor then vanished into thin air! I was stunned into silence and sat there in complete shock! Did that just happen? I am not asleep; I am not intoxicated as I hadn't had a drink in three weeks since the hospital trip; am I dreaming? Nope, nope, and nope! I am sitting here wide awake in my bed and I just saw a thing break into a billion particles and disappear into thin air! WOW! I gave my head a shake, rubbed my eyes and then fear kicked me into motion. I leaped out of bed and ran past the place where that thing or "Angel of Death" was standing and felt a wave of icy, cold, dark air rush past me. The thickness of it as well as the rancid smell almost made me vomit. I cannot put into words the feelings I had as I ran down the hall in my pyjamas and bare feet across the street to my good friend's place. I pounded on his door and stayed with him on the couch for the rest of the night, recounting the incredible experience I just had and very close call with the Angel of Death! I thought for sure he would mock me and not believe this incredible tale, but he did believe me because he told me a similar experience he had as well quite some time ago. He never spoke about it because he was sure nobody would believe him either. Well at least I wasn't alone in this almost surreal experience! If anything, this whole incident made me realize just how precious the cord of life is and I vowed right then and there to *never* play with it again. WOW! I just had an insight to the other side of life and recognized just how very close we are to it. There is a very fine line between worlds and I saw only a glimpse of it and that was good enough for me. My imagination ran wild and I could envision the fires of hell and the beasts that accompany it...no thank you. I will take God's Grace over the evils of the world any day.

It was right after this episode that I started school in Hinton and met my future husband and father to my only daughter. Things had moved very fast with our courtship and before I knew it, I was pregnant. Great! Just great! This threw me completely off as I was only 23 and having a child when I was finally having thoughts about going to college didn't exactly work into my new plans. At first I really wasn't sure about the whole pregnancy idea as it came rather unexpected, but then I had a powerful dream that sealed my decision with motherhood and my future.

I dreamt there was a bright, white light where a deep voice was coming out of it saying: "You *MUST* have this child as it has a very special mission in life to accomplish and it needs to be born unto you Kathy. This Soul *MUST* be born!" I woke up completely shaken as the voice was so very loud and real not to mention the Light that was so very bright and incredibly uplifting! I truly felt that God had spoken to me, so who was I to argue with God? I said ok and decided to give this baby all the love I had in me – and that was lots!

Being pregnant was by far the best feeling I have ever experienced; I felt the beauty radiate from me. I loved feeling the baby move inside me and thrilled at the fact of being a mom and finally being able to give all of my love to this beautiful Soul growing inside me. I finished my GED and felt good about that accomplishment, but still wanted more education to follow as I now had the self-confidence and the hope that I could actually achieve something with my life. It had never occurred to me once before about going to college, but now the idea was very appealing to me. I realized I was actually quite smart and was very interested in school. However, the schooling would have to wait because I developed some complications with the pregnancy and had to spend a month and a half in the hospital in Edmonton on bedrest. My daughter was born by cesarean section a month and a half early due to these complications, so her lungs were not fully developed, and she had to be admitted to Neonatal Intensive Care Unit at the University of Alberta Hospital.

On the third day of life, amidst all the tubing and lifelines, the nurse asked me to try to give her an ounce of milk for the first time to see how she would react to it. As I prepared to do so, Tanis, my daughter, was lying on her back looking up at me. Her black little eyes looked at me then drifted off to where the nurse was standing, then back to me. I was distracted by the nurse leaving, and as I turned around to attempt to give her a mini bottle of milk, I looked at her and saw two distinct blue lights in the form of stars come into her eyes and with it, a recognition of a Soul I had been with before! I dropped the bottle and gasped: "I KNOW YOU!" I had recognized her from long, long ago is the only way to put it. How is that possible when she was just born? The look in her eyes was that of a Soul I seemed to have known for a very long time. She was an "Old Soul" in the form of a newborn babe…if that makes sense. I knew this baby with all my heart and Soul! It was then that I understood that from that moment on, everything would be just fine. With that, the starry blue lights disappeared and she was back to having black eyes. That very day, to the doctors' disbelief, she suddenly didn't require any more massive action on their part; she just needed to gain some weight so I could take her home, which I did 2 weeks later.

Although I truly loved being married and being a mom to two incredible beautiful young girls (he had a beautiful daughter from a previous relationship), the marriage just was not to be. We had two very different goals in life, and mine was not to spend the rest of my days in Hinton, Alberta. We had moved to Edmonton to see if it could work out there, but it just was not to be. We separated and filed for divorce. He took his daughter with him and I had Tanis with me. It was a very difficult split as he would no longer allow me to see his little girl whom I had raised as my own, and this completely broke my heart. It was a deep pain that tore me apart, but I recognized that one day she would grow up and I could explain it to her. The loss of losing a child I raised like my own was a very painful and difficult time for me and added to my list of pains in life...another tic on the sheet of hardships.

Finding myself alone with my daughter, I decided I needed a career other than working as a receptionist (which I absolutely despised) so I would be able to encourage my daughter to do the same one day. I found out that the Edmonton General Hospital was hiring Nursing Attendants and paid $10/hour, more than I was making at the time as a receptionist; answering phones is just not my cup of tea either. Although I had zero experience or education in the health field, the determination to get a better paying job as a single mom pushed me to apply at the Edmonton General Hospital every Friday for 3 months straight. They finally gave me an interview just to see why in the world I was applying for a job I wasn't qualified for. I flat out told them that I was perfect for the job because of the kind and loving person I was. I knew I was very capable of it and if they would give me a chance, I would prove it! Well, they did give me chance. They told me to come in the following day so I could shadow another worker, and if I did well then we would talk about a possible job. I outshined everyone there and was hired immediately! Not only did they give me a job, but they paid for the $2000.00 course it took to get the Nursing Attendant Certificate! How is that for awesome? See what determination will do? Persistence even in the face of adversity? Never give up and just keep at it even when the odds are against you!

It didn't take me long to figure out that there was more to my career than being a nursing attendant. I applied to school to become a Licensed Practical Nurse and was accepted. Thus began the struggle to go to school, work part-time and be a single mom of a 3-year-old. I did it and graduated nursing in 1998 with my diploma. It was the happiest day of my life other than my daughter being born. I had finally left the nastiness of my past way behind me and I was on my way to being successful in the nursing field. I took regular trips into the mountains to rejuvenate my energies and truly believed my life was under control. Nothing could stop me now, or so I thought because I was well on my way to a great and adventuresome life.

Life was great when I took a job in the Diabetic Foot Clinic for the first year. After that, things became increasingly difficult to manage as finding a babysitter became an issue. I asked my mother to move in with me to assist me while I worked the evening position on an Orthopedics Unit. I thought that moving in with me would help her as life always seemed so difficult and really didn't need to be this way. I promised to help her find a job, then an apartment so she could finally for once live a happy and productive life. She was happy to be here with me, but life slowly started to dwindle before my very eyes. The layer of happiness I thought I had started to show signs of stress and was cracking at the seams simply because I didn't have a foundation of what life was really about. I had lived an illusion my entire life and had no real idea or teachings of what to do when times get tough.

What I have come to understand now is that beneath the layer of happiness of my life, all the undealt pain and trauma was still festering and growing strength. All the extreme insecurities and pain I had lived since I was a child had never been talked about or looked at, so the very second problems came my way, my low self-esteem that was masked underneath a veil of happiness, kicked in with full force. I did what I could to survive and did my best with what life threw at me. My inability to handle problems or cope with life in general suddenly showed their nasty face, and my solution was to drink alcohol to relieve the pressure. I began to drink with my mother almost every day, even if it was just a little bit. Little did I know, this was to be the beginning of a 10-year drinking career that would lead to disaster, and a life full of shame topped off by guilt.

Before the drinking began, I had a dream that has stayed with me my entire life due to the extreme realness and significance of it. Although I have had many dreams of great importance throughout the years leading me to gain an understanding of what was going on in my life, it was during this highlight of my life that I had the ULTIMATE dream experience. It goes like this: I was standing in a desert by a Holy Temple that had a roof in the shape of a pyramid. There was a smiling bald man sitting in the front of the Temple, but he seemed to have no legs, or if he did he sure couldn't use them to walk. He had the most sparkling, blue eyes I had ever seen that appeared to twinkle at me in amusement. He invited me into the Temple but I decided to go back into the desert to go look for something. He advised me to not do that as it was a bad idea. I insisted that I would be back and turned to step into the sand. He looked at me sadly and shook his head as if to say I had failed a test. To my utter surprise, he stood up and turned around to walk back into the Temple. By now the sand had become like cement and I could no longer move in any direction. As I was berating myself for not listening to the wise man, I heard a groaning behind me that didn't sound of this world. I turned my upper body around to get a peek and saw an endless lineup of Zombie like men heading towards me. Their eyes were only deep, dark, empty sockets and their body's void of a Soul.

Before I knew it and to my horror, they were upon me and were trying to attack me. I instantly screamed, "NO!" and became invisible instantly disappearing out of sight (a trick I had learned as a teenager and use it regularly in my dreams). The zombie that was on top of me was howling with rage unable to detect where I had disappeared to. I found myself in the Temple lying in a triangular cubicle, lying face up. I could see an incredible bright white light at the end where my feet were. It seemed to move and pulsate to a rhythm of a vibrational Sound I could not detect. I cried out: "YES!" and was pulled into the vortex of this incredible Light which I presumed to be of God. I hung in the middle of it and was being purified and cleansed of all negative energy in and around me. With a kiss from Heaven, I was wrapped in the loving arms of God! I hung in a golden vortex filling myself with a Love so pure that it molded Itself into my every atom. I was lifted higher and higher as the cleansing and purification continued. The vibrational effect was pulsating through my entire sheath of a body that I didn't really have, as I consisted on only a glowing see through consistency.

All of a sudden, I was thrust out of this LIGHT into a black vortex where no time existed. I wasn't even a speck; I just was. In this sacred place, there was nothing but my consciousness and the Presence of

God! Words cannot describe the world I was in nor the incredulous experience I was given! At the same time this was happening, I could feel my physical body that was lying on the couch in my apartment having a nap. I could feel my body tingling all over at the same time I was hanging in out in space with nothing but a consciousness. I had dual perceptions at the same time! I suddenly awoke with a start as if I had fallen into my body from up high. It was by far the most amazing experience ever given to me. For the longest time after this vivid dream, I would tingle all over when I re-lived the power of it. Wow! What an incredible gift I received and to this day am grateful because in my moments of doubt, I think of it and my Faith is renewed instantly. This powerful dream actually helped me through the next 7 years of hell that I was unknowingly embarking on. It gave me the belief that I had the inner strength and resources to fight my way through the negative blackness that constantly surrounded my every waking moment. I was able to relive this dream, and find courage and mostly *HOPE* through the powerful force of the Light of God.

Even though there were many times that I truly believed I would not live the day, I knew deep in my heart that a power much greater than myself did in fact exist; that even if I died, I had already experienced this wondrous existence that defied any physical understandings. I knew that when I died whether it be with the current situation I was stuck in or later on in life, it didn't matter because I had witnessed and experienced but a mere glimpse of what was on the other side of the curtain. I held no more fear of death. If anything, this dream gave me an understanding of the death of the physical body, and that there is life when we leave this temple of a body we temporarily call home. I was now armed with a knowledge that I would be protected from this day forth and my view on life would never be the same again.

Hope is an interesting thing. While it is alive in your heart, it can pulsate and put a skip in your step. However, when you don't have it, the world can quickly become a dark and dreary place to reside in. It drains the life right out of you and takes away all motivation to live; purpose seems to suddenly vanish into thin air. Poof, and it's gone! Getting up in the morning or even getting dressed and combing your hair can become a chore if you have no reason to get up; no hopeful aspirations for the coming day. The "Blah" feeling sets in and before you know it, a depressive state can mould itself to your inner being without you even realising it's there. Nothing will appeal to you; not the sun shining outside, nor the birds singing, nor the happiness of your surrounding family. Nothing will help you get out of that state of mind unless a tiny grain of Hope resides deep inside you somewhere. A seed is all you need to have Hope grow into a life of its own. It is something that requires nurturing and constant care, and you are the only one who can bring it to life. You are probably wondering: "How do I accomplish that when all odds are against me? Where do I find Hope in a world filled with darkness, pain and suffering?" The answer to that lies within yourself. No one can put it into motion for you. You have to push yourself to go out there, in that big, bad world, and find the resources necessary to help you help yourself get out of the rut you may be in. Local libraries have all sorts of resources available, counselling, journaling your deepest innermost thoughts, pushing yourself to get outside when you don't feel like it, yoga, volunteering in a place such as brain injury rehab unit, will show you that other people face more hardships in life, and that maybe there are some positives in your life after all.

Like I have written earlier, if you continuously dwell on the negatives in your life, then you will experience only negatives and tell yourself that life sucks. You are the only one that creates your reality, so the choice is ultimately yours. Negative or positive? I fully understand the great difficulty to try and see positive when surrounded by negativity, but the key is to tell yourself that whatever you are presently experiencing will come to pass. It is only temporary. It's the cycle of life; it will not rain every single day of your life! Tornadoes may come and go, but the sun will come out to shine and give you a rainbow, maybe even two, so you have to prepare yourself for that glorious moment in time that is awaiting you with open arms.

Make yourself a list of all the negatives on one side of the sheet, then all the positives on the other side of the sheet. Even if there is a very long list of negatives and few positives, date it and keep that list as a reminder of what you need to work on. Use it as a motivating tool to get you to move a step closer to feeling better about yourself. Prioritize them by numbers of what it is that needs work first such as removing toxic people from your life. This is a great number one on your list. Take a long, hard look at who you surround yourself with; are they goal oriented or do they have nothing to contribute but bad jokes and empty words? Do they put others down, laugh at others or mock people? Or are they the kind of person that will help others when needed, be kind and caring? Really analyze who in is in your immediate circle of friends and decide who will help you attain your goals and who will only serve as an anchor? Work your way down the list and you will already feel better because at least you have taken a step in helping yourself eliminate the negatives. When it comes to the positives, you may tell yourself there are none. Baloney! There is always a positive! You are breathing so there's a positive right off the bat! Do you have your health? Do you a roof over your head? Do you have a little food in your fridge? It's the little things we tend to take for granted and we forget that really are a positive in our life. Which ones do you have?

Setting a goal will give you hope and something tangible to work towards. If you don't have goals, then ask yourself why should you even bother getting out of bed? It doesn't matter what life throws at you, make yourself a small, attainable goal that you can reach easily, then make a harder one the next time. So on and so forth. One day at a time; one hour at a time; one minute at a time; one step at a time.

"Hope is a waking dream"
~Aristotle~

STOP AND REFLECT:

1. What has been going on in your life that has given you a shred of Hope?

_____

_____

_____

_____

_____

2. What does Hope mean to you? Has it helped you get through the hard times?

_____

_____

_____

_____

3. Have you ever felt as if there were no Hope? Why?

_____

_____

_____

_____

4. How do you find Hope in world that sometimes seems filled with Hopelessness?

_____

_____

_____

_____

_____

5. Hope can come in the form of many faces. What measures can you take today to find Hope in whatever difficult situation you may be facing right now?

_____

_____

_____

_____

_____

Top:
Molested until the age of 4 by the
foster father where I was living.

Bottom:
Tied to a chair in the neighbors
garage and beaten/molested by
the boys next door. Step-dad
beat me for "lying" to him about
the blood and torn clothes.

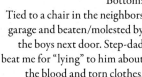

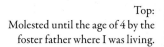

Top:
Forced to have sex at 14
by my first boyfriend

Bottom and Across:
First modelling pictures in
Montreal at the age of 18.

Drugged and raped by a photographer in Miami at 18 yrs old

New York Modelling pictures

▮MAKEOVER▮

r oots: the saga continues

Model Kristelle Desgagne wanted to rediscover her hair-itage. So we showed her how to get rid of those brassy blond locks and return to her natural light brown roots

When Kristelle Desgagne came to our SEVENTEEN offices, she knew there was no turning back. "My hair's a mess," groaned the twenty-year-old model. "It's overprocessed and under-

BEFORE

AFTER

styled." No problem—we knew just what to do. In no time our beauty editors took Kristelle to New York's Bumble + Bumble salon and introduced her to colorist Shari Glindman and hairstylist Alberto Guzman. Then came the cut and coloring: 1. First Alberto reshaped Kristelle's layers to add fullness to her fine hair. Then, to create a soft, feminine feel, he trimmed her bangs and top layers just

slightly. Next, Alberto reshaped Kristelle's hair on the sides to softly frame her face and show off her classically beautiful features. Short layers were also added in back, near the nape of the neck, to give her hair a bit of texture—without making it look too boyish. 2. To rediscover Kristelle's true hue, colorist Shari applied a natural henna treatment to give her hair warmth and help it absorb the new color. 3. Next, to keep the color consistent, Shari applied a tint that matched Kristelle's light brown roots. 4. Since the hair coloring muted Kristelle's natural highlights and left her

hair looking dull and drab, Shari brightened things up with a bit of creative hair painting (randomly coloring strands of hair to create a natural, sun-kissed look). 5. The fabulous final result: a toned-down golden-brown hair color that perfectly complements Kristelle's new 'do. "I'm so happy with the results," says Kristelle. "My hair's never looked this shiny before. This is the *real me* coming through."

Seventeen—April 2000

18 years old

←

42 years old

→

102

Top:
My best friend Tasha who
stood by me through all the
rough times. She loved me like
a sister and to this day, I am
grateful for her loving support!

Bottom:
Graduation Class 1998

Tanis made this card for me while we stayed in the Whitehorse Women's Shelter. I was still working at the hospital nursing It took me 3 days to come to the decision to send her to her dad's for her own safety. Hardest thing I ever did!

To: Mom

Hey mom,
I wont you to decide what's best for you, and I wont be mad at you. I respect your decision mom. I know that you'll pick what's right.

From: Tanis Lisdahl-ski

I Love you mom

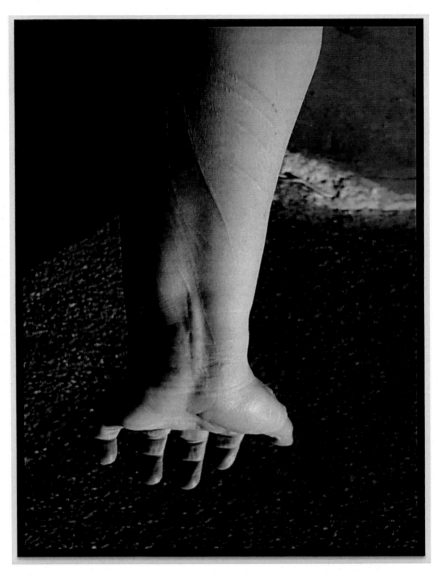

I self-harmed, induced by alcohol abuse, toxic relationships and my inability to cope. It was shortly after this I was evicted, lost my nursing career, my daughter refused to talk to me and I became homeless with no hope.

Top:
When you feel
like quitting;
think about why
you started...

Bottom:
We are Goats!!!!
Best hiking trip
ever at Miette Hot
Springs Resort.

Bottom:
Dozer Training with
Women Building
Futures - 2013

The Love of my life! Roland - my Ebenezer - my ROCK!

Top:
Work Boot Recycling
Program I started in
2014 - over 1700 pairs
of gently used boots
distributed to Safety
Programs who offer
FREE Safety Tickets
to those struggling to
get their lives back.

Bottom:
Operation Hydration
that I started in 2013
giving ice cold water
to the homeless on the
hottest days of the year.

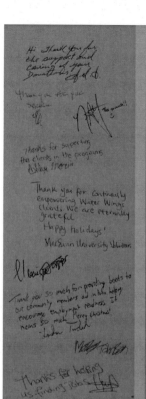

Hi Thank you for
the support and
caring of your
Donations...

Thank you for you...

Thanks for supporting
the clients in the programs

Thank you for continuously
empowering Water Wings
Clients. We are eternally
grateful
Happy Holidays!
MacEwan University Volunteers

Thank you so much for providing boots to
our community members and in turn helping
encourage employment readiness. It
means so much. Merry Christmas!

Thanks for helping
us finding jobs

Thank you for
your support!
Have a nice Holiday
and Holidays

CHANGING PEOPLE'S L

Getting back into the workforc
many of our community mem
often means that individual wo
finances upfront to cover bus
Approximately 10 years ago
distributing steel-toed work be
able to provide a letter from th
approximately 45 work boots a
a year by helping them get bac
financial hardship of purchasin

As someone who understood
work boots for a job, Imperial
boot drive that helped supply
agencies around the inner city
this program.

"It will change a person's life.
really struggling and the barrie
their family is just a pair of boo
to be able to get those boots,"

After noticing a pair of work boo
in a garbage bin, Kathy took it u
at Imperial's Kearl Oil Sands pro
who would truly benefit from t

"I asked my managers if I could
aside or aren't being used. They
450 pairs!"

With the success of her recyc
installed permanent recycle bi
boots.

"I am going to do this drive ag
site-wide at our different locat
up I am hoping to get more thi

Thanks so much for
the boots! John...

To: Kathy – Our Safety Boots 'Angel'
"No boots... no job!" Your project is
essential to our clients! "We were thrilled the day
you walked through our doors! Many thanks –
Eric Rushing,
Water Wings Edmonton

To: Todd Mc
Imperial
Thank you for y
boots! Best re

Thanks from Water Wings. Your
donations of steel toe boots are greatly
appreciated.

Thank you for supporting
this program

VES ONE STEP AT A TIME

...netimes a catch twenty two for
...landing a temp job for the day
...ady need to have the necessary
...work clothing, and even lunch.
...stard Seed Edmonton began
...ommunity members who were
...loyer. This program distributes
...and assists over 500 individuals
...e work force without the added
...approved steel-toed boots.

...dship of purchasing items like
...e Kathy initiated a yearly work
...tard Seed Edmonton and other
...e necessary boots they need for

...or a fact that when a person is
...stopping them from supporting
...big of a stepping stone it is just
...ay.

...r pristine condition thrown away
...self to encourage her coworkers
...onate their used boots to others

...nd recycle boots that are tossed
...olutely, so last year we collected

...c boot drive, Kathy's managers
...e people can leave their excess

...ay and have recycle bins placed
...th construction season coming
...aid Kathy.

We really appreciate your
kindness in donating boots to us!
John Kute

Glory Odurkwa
Well done
keep it up

Thanks for
supporting our clients.
Corina

Hi Kathy, the services
you sended to Imagees
don't have the PPE, but want to
is greatly appreciated.
Thank you and enjoy
the holiday season
Joe ? numbir

Abdirahman Aliawal

Thanks for your
Service.
Thanks
Edwin Bwoga

KH12 ...

Thanks so much
for your support.
Merry xmas Bob Hawey

Thank you very much you generous
offer has help so much Happy holiday
-Andrew Dancey

...d & Paul Ferguson,

...enerous donation of safety
...Eric Bishop - Water Wings
Edmonton

Our students are poor and
cannot afford steel-toe
boots. Your donations help
them to work safely. Thanks
Joe
Water Wings
Co-worker

Thanks so much for your Help

THANKS FOR YOUR DONATIONS
HAPPY HOLIDAYS

Thank you so much for your help.
I am very grateful that you gave
me a chance :)
Happy Holidays :)

Top:
797F Caterpillar 385+ Metric tonne Heavy Haul Truck - my "Baby"

Bottom:
208,000L water truck that I drive to keep the dust down
during the hot summer days in the mine.

Working safely is everything to me! This job has changed me forever and I hope to show all women out there that careers in the trades are men's best kept secret! Take a step no matter your age and give yourself a chance. I did!

Chapter 6:

BIRD WITH A BROKEN WING

Personal Boundaries/Codependency:

Personal boundaries are guidelines, rules or limits that a person creates to identify reasonable, safe and permissible ways for other people to behave towards them and how they will respond when someone passes those limits. They are built out of a mix of conclusions, beliefs, opinions, attitudes, past experiences and social learning. Personal boundaries help to define an individual by outlining likes and dislikes, and setting the distances one allows others to approach. They include physical, mental, psychological and spiritual boundaries, involving beliefs, emotions, intuitions and self-esteem. Personal boundaries operate in two directions, affecting both the incoming and outgoing interactions between people.

Codependency

Codependency often involves placing a lower priority on one's own needs, while being excessively preoccupied with the needs of others. Codependency can occur in any type of relationship, including family, work, friendship, and also romantic, peer or community relationships. While a healthy relationship depends on the emotional space provided by personal boundaries, co-dependent personalities have difficulties in setting such limits, so that defining and protecting boundaries efficiently may be for them a vital part of regaining mental health. In a codependent relationship, the codependent's sense of purpose is based on making extreme sacrifices to satisfy their partner's needs. Codependent relationships signify a degree of unhealthy clinginess, where one person doesn't have self-sufficiency or autonomy. One or both parties depend on the other for fulfillment. There is usually an unconscious reason for continuing to put another person's life first, often for the mistaken notion that self-worth comes from other people.[7]

Vulnerability

Everything and everyone is susceptible to vulnerability at one time of another, be it at different stages and degrees. Thus it is important to understand the basics of vulnerability. Often described as the susceptibility of an individual, group, society or system to emotional or physical changes made either indirectly or directly impacting the fore mentioned.

When a certain situation presents itself the individual, group or system responding to that particular scenario is often dictated by the allowance or manipulation depicted within the relaxing or leeway given towards the outcome.

When this relaxed or unguarded frame is introduced into the scenario, it often contributes to the manipulation, persuasion, temptation or any other factors which eventually produces the vulnerability state. This state of vulnerability opens the focus for censure, criticism and unfounded blaming exercises.

---

7   From Wikipedia, the free encyclopedia

Where do I even start? This subject matter is such a deep one; I sadly never even learned these words until I was 40 and had to take time off of life in order to mend the brokenness within me. I truly did not know the meaning of boundaries or codependency, nor did I realize just how vulnerable or naïve I really was. I actually had to ask the definitions from my counselor. You mean I can say "NO" and not feel guilty? What? How come no one ever told me about this before the age of 40? You mean I don't have to be a doormat for everyone to put their dirty feet all over me and step on me? Where have I been my entire life? Asleep and in a complete fog...that's where! The difference in me since I learned how to include the simple word "NO" into my vocabulary has been life altering, and I am not kidding about that. The freedom I now feel in comparison to before extends from either end of the spectrum. One cannot compare to the newfound freedom of expression simply by a two letter word.

I believe that due to the extreme conditions I endured as a child and continuing on as a teenager, the notion that I had a choice with my personal space was completely lost on me. I had no voice in my own story called life, so my personal space was infringed upon for most of my life. How can a person be so caught up inside that they cannot even speak up when another person is pushing themselves into their space? The inner battle of misery and rage that was going on inside me remained unspoken for 40 years. An overwhelming feeling of obligation to let others always have their way; too terrified to say what I was truly feeling is a very sad way of living to say the least. Learning about boundaries and codependency was by far the best thing that I could have ever been shown. My self-worth was entirely based on what others thought of me; it never occurred to me once of what did *I* think of me? I was so focused on trying to please others and have them love me and want me, that I would do almost anything for their time, attention and affection. The term "Starving for Love" was exactly how I was, thus all my actions, thoughts and deeds helped me to create a Kathy that everybody would love to love. It was hard for me to rid myself of this old habit and learn to just be ME! I didn't even know who that was.

Boundaries are such an important part of life and a necessity I must add. Without them, a person becomes a doormat and runs themselves ragged trying to please every person in the room but themselves. People with no boundaries become unsure about when it is appropriate to say no and set limits. They find it difficult to take ownership of their choices, freedom, and responsibilities. They simply cannot say "no" even when they don't have the time or energy to do what was asked of them. They will say "yes" regardless of how they feel, and most cases put themselves on the back burner left burning the candle at both ends, until one day they crash into a brick wall of exhaustion. Just like I did. Being able to recognize when your needs come first is a huge step in a suffering person's life. This is extremely difficult in any caregiver's life because the obligation of taking care of a sick child, elderly parent or spouse.

Illness in a family member is often the major player in us forgetting our own needs as well. The sheer guilt trip we often endure due to this will keep us pushing against the grain and push ourselves to the limit of exhaustion. The preoccupation of the other person's condition often makes us think that they need more than we do, but in reality if we do not learn to take the time necessary to care for ourselves first and foremost, how in the world are we supposed to care for another human being? I never understood this as I always put everyone else's needs way before mine, and in nursing, this was very easy for me to do. I figured my problems were not nearly as bad as the people lying sick and dying horrible deaths in the hospital so who was I to complain about a few bruises and name calling? This is where I was so very, very wrong. When I say that our needs must come first, I do not mean in a selfish, excessive sort of way. I mean that if I am exhausted and someone wants me to go clean their house because they are ill, I need to be able to tell them that I am tired and need my rest first...*then and only then* will I be able to go help them out regardless of whatever guilt trip they try to lay on you.

Standing firm in your decision is an important factor in learning to establish your own boundaries. The more you are lenient with your boundaries, the more people around you know it and will use it repeatedly to encroach their needs in your time and space. Pay attention to the blood sucking life drainers, energy robbers and the negative, toxic people around you. If you cannot rid yourself of them, then at least limit your time with them regardless of what they say. Slowly surround yourself with people that will lift you up; not bring you down. This can be extremely difficult when these negative people are in your immediate family, but regardless, boundaries *need* to be firmly established if you want any peace of mind. I had to learn the extremely long and hard way about this, so I will share some of my experiences with you in hopes you don't follow the same path and learn from my mistakes in life.

When you have low self-worth and rely solely on others opinions to feed your ego, your standards fall below what you would normally tolerate if you had a healthy self-esteem. What you tolerate is what will continue; don't ever forget that! The more you feel crappy about yourself, the more you will tolerate negative input from others and this can often lead to abusive situations. At first it may show up as negative comments regarding the way you cook food, or the way you look and dress, wear makeup or comb your hair. The negative comments will make you think that maybe you should take cooking lessons, that you do wear too much makeup and that your clothes and hair are a mess or that everything about you is wrong. All these said things can make you re-evaluate yourself and how you are in the eyes of the one who says he "loves you". STOP RIGHT THERE! If this is the case that is going on in your life, then I strongly suggest you take a long, hard look at yourself and what it is you are looking for in this person. Is the opinion of another worth more to you than your own? If you have a healthy self-esteem you will be able to say, "Well buddy, this is the way I am and if you are not happy with it, then you can go find another person who is better suited to your tastes." It's one thing to be having a bad hair day and a completely another to be constantly told everything about us is wrong. If you are basing your self-worth on what another person is telling you, then maybe it's time to look at *yourself first* to see *why* is it so important for someone else to like you? If there is something you don't like about yourself, then begin to work on it to make it better for *yourself – not another person's ideas of how you should be!* This is very crucial to setting healthy boundaries. If someone is telling you to change this and change that, ask yourself why? If they are having such a difficult time with the way you are, then why are they with you to begin with? People misuse the word "Love" all the time. They mistreat you but say they love you; this is *NOT* love! Remind yourself of that! Love is patient; love is kind, Love is good and uplifting NOT berating and degrading nor humiliating!

My drinking only escalated with my inability to cope with life. I was going to school full time and working part time at the hospital while still trying to deal with things at home. I had zero positive outlets and drinking alcohol became my best friend. This led to my making many, many, many bad decisions while in the intoxicated state of mind. The number one on that long list was bringing my very first boyfriend who had hurt me when I was a 14, come for a visit over Christmas. When it comes to bad ideas, that one tops the list! What was I thinking? Oh yeah....I was drinking and NOT thinking! He had gotten my phone number somehow and while I was intoxicated, he easily wooed me into believing he had changed over the years and wanted to see me desperately. Because I grew up with him, I felt a connection that at least he understood me and I believed his promises of help. He convinced me that he was here to help me and things would be good. That was by far the worst decision I ever made was to have him come for a "visit". That intoxicated decision cost me 3 years of intense violence, trauma and much pain.

There is too much to say here about the intensity of the situation; besides, what more can be said about violence and abuse? After his 2 weeks were up, I knew he had to go back to Quebec and fast! I was waiting for the day when his return ticket to Quebec would come, but then he went and burned it then told me he wasn't going anywhere...all hope drained right out of me in that very instant! Instead of reacting in the normal way and simply calling the airlines to get another one, I felt trapped and unable to voice my thoughts on the matter. I felt completely vulnerable and decided to make the best of the situation at hand seeing as I felt I had no choice in the matter. Do you see how my thought pattern was mixed up? *I DID HAVE A CHOICE!* I truly did not *Recognize* It, though! I was unable to see that all I had to do was stand my ground and get him on that plane at all costs. I truly didn't see a way out of the situation, not even calling the airlines to replace the ticket! That is just how limited my vision was at the time. My inability to take a stand for myself and set boundaries had led me down a path of violence and destruction that lasted for the better part of 3 years. All it would have taken was for me to say, "No! You are getting on that plane or I am calling the police to escort you there!" But I was unable to utter 2 words because I was so traumatized by attempting to voice my thoughts and being met only with harsh words, violence and disdain. Instead, I took the alternate route and decided to make the best of the situation at hand and figure out something at a later date. The mental breakdown to come was catastrophic in completely destroying whatever self-esteem I thought I may have had.

I had always been slim, but during this time I gained 100 lbs in one year's time and was left in a physical state of complete and utter distress. This weight gain tore down whatever I had in reserves of feeling good about myself. It was here that I realized just how empty of a shell I really was all along. I had spent my entire life relying on my physical looks and body image to get what I had wanted out of life. Beauty had been a means of manipulating to obtain whatever I wanted and sadly, I used it mercilessly. I truly believed that physical beauty was what was important in life and without it, I was nothing. Take that precious gift of good looks away and now I had nothing to fall back on. I was left an overweight, drunk, empty shell of a person who was drinking way too much to relieve the inner turmoil and pain. The alcohol gave me the strength to endure the situation I was in...or so I told myself. It made me feel better about myself and not care if I was fat and undesirable anymore. The alcohol, on the other hand, made him even more of an animal of destruction. The physical and verbal abuse only escalated, making work my escape, but even that was becoming increasingly difficult to hide the bruises and misery I was living. I alienated myself from all other staff and focused solely on the patients and giving them as much love as I could. Their problems seemed so much worse than mine, so I would downplay my situation at home to *"not that bad"* when really *it was that bad!*

He used to sleep in front of the door of the apartment so I could not escape him. He would follow me to work and make sure he was there on my lunch breaks as well as after work. He would ensure his physical presence was known to me and that he knew at all times where I was and what I was doing. I had no time to collect my thoughts and try to plan an escape. The few times I did manage to put him in jail for assault, he would convince me to bail him out because he didn't speak any English and how could I possibly leave him in that situation? His promises of never doing it again only lasted until the next time he drank, then it would start all over again. One time he held me under a cold shower for 30 minutes so I would learn to think clearly. How insane is that?

After moving a few times to different cities to try to escape him, I finally decided the only way I would be rid of this monster in disguise was to go back to Quebec where at least I had family support and he had his. He would be back in his domain and would be able to find work since he had been living off of me for the last 2 years, this was my only solution. I pretended that we would go back and make a try at it there, when really my plan was to get him the heck away from me with my family as backup and help. My poor daughter was caught up in all of this as I truly tried to make the best of the situation at hand. Guilt piled on top of guilt became my best friend accompanied by alcohol.

I sold everything I had and loaded up the bare necessities in an old 1973 Econoline blue "Cheech & Chong" van and began my trek across Canada from Terrace, BC to Val D'Or, Quebec a grand total of 4,359.5 km. How we made it there with only a flat tire and plugged fuel filter remains a mystery to me! Divine Intervention is more like it because when we got that van inspected for Out of Province Insurance purposes, the mechanic refused to let us drive out of the shop. He gave us a list that was a page long of all that was mechanically wrong with it, including a cracked frame! We were truly looked after indeed and what a Blessing!

The violence only escalated once we got there because he fell back into drugs and the insanity only intensified. One night on St-Jean Baptist, Quebec's national birthday, I left the bonfire and celebrations because I just didn't want to be surrounded by drunken idiots, so I went home. I woke up to being beaten and raped by this animal who was demonic in his enjoyment of my pain and torment. I heard movement in the other room and I realized an old boyfriend of my sister's had come to sleep on the couch for the night. He heard what was going on in the bedroom as the door was wide open for him to witness it firsthand. The beast that was on top of me punching me as he violently raped me, was screaming like a madman how I was a slut and I wanted for both of them to get on me. The "friend" that I have known since childhood, saw my predicament as I am yelling at him to help me, looked at me directly in the eyes and shook his head as if to say, "Sorry...I can't help you," and walked out the door leaving me to endure a night of torture and hell on earth with a madman. How could this person who went out with my very own sister not help me in a time of need? How could he just leave me to be beaten to a pulp and hurt beyond any words? I still can see the clear betrayal in his blue eyes and the cowardice of not wanting to get involved and it has stayed with me until this day. Wow! That night was a very long and painful one and it took me quite a while to get over that one not only physically but emotionally as well.

When I finally managed to put him in jail for assault and battery and move to another town, I thought things would be good and I could start over. But one sunny day as I am making breakfast for my daughter and her friend, that peace was taken away from me in a split second. The door was open as the sun was shining and I was feeling really good, until I heard a voice in the doorway. Time stopped as I recognized the voice and was instantly paralyzed with deep, intense fear. Never mind fear trickling through my veins...it was a full on flooding! I could hear my heart pounding in my ears like a roaring river yet I couldn't breathe nor move. I felt a need to urinate and almost did right there out of sheer fright! I was in my pyjamas in the dining room at the top of the staircase of the split-level duplex, and saw him standing in the frame of the open doorway looking at me with the evilest sneer I had ever witnessed. My only thoughts were: "He's going to kill me and the damn phone is downstairs; I will never be able to make it there to call 911!" When did he get out of jail and how the *HELL* did he find me?" These thoughts raced through my mind as I am trying to think at the same time of where to put my daughter and her friend in safety without witnessing the violence to come. I still was unable to move or speak and was literally frozen to the spot. Time had seemingly stopped with everything happening in slow motion. Surprisingly, all he did was laugh at me and tell me that all he wanted was to let me know that he knew where I lived, and that he would be back to get me when I least expected it. He was coming for me were his exact words; only I wouldn't know when! With a sadistic laugh that still sends shivers down my spine, he turned and left. I suddenly found my footing and ran down the stairs to slam the door shut and lock it. Tears flowed as I envisioned all sorts of bad scenarios to come. Without a second thought, I knew I was going back to the safety of Alberta. I applied online and was hired immediately at the University of Alberta

Hospital. I called my friend long time Tasha whom I went to nursing school with (whose picture is featured in the middle of the book) for help with finding a place to live and I started packing. I left there in the blink of an eye, giving away most of my stuff and only packing the absolutely necessary things needed. Getting to the train in Montreal was an absolute nightmare that I won't get into, but I finally made it to safety with my daughter, my beloved dog, and 10 boxes. The rest of my boxes ready to be shipped at a later date remained at my sister's for the time being. I would never see them again as her idiot boyfriend blew the house up and I lost everything I owned! Mind you...so did she.

Starting over in Alberta was easy; the problem was that I was a complete mess from the last 3 years of horrible violence and abuse in all forms. Tasha had given me her spare room to have with my daughter until I could get settled in my own place. Her help was simply priceless to me; from the time she picked me up with my 10 boxes and my dog included, to helping me find a place to stay, getting all my nursing papers in order and just being there for me as I transitioned into a new life (again). Thank you for all that you have done for me Tasha; you helped me more than you will ever know and I am eternally grateful.

I was trying to work, be a single mom and start over with nothing and all that with a damaged mind. I was so very tired but still needed to push on but having zero coping skills I did what I only knew how to respond to stress; drink. I ended up hanging out after work in a bar where not so nice people would prey on vulnerable people such as myself. Not being in the healthiest state of mind, my decision making skills led me to end up being wooed by a man who promised me all sorts of good things to help me out. My mistake was believing he could save me from a difficult situation. I didn't realize back then that I was the one responsible for saving myself and that no-one else could do it for me. I was co-dependent now and relied on others to help me get out the mess I was in while still pretending to be holding up ok. The regular alcohol intake made my judgment and decision making not the best, to say the least. I went from a struggling bad situation, to one that was way worse by far. I jumped from one boiling pot of water directly into the fires of hell! The next 4 years would bring me to the brink of death many a time. I had no idea that fear could get worse bringing you to the deepest and darkest places that exist in your mind and on earth.

The promises made proved to be all false hope and before I could bat an eye, I found myself in a situation where there was no escape. I found out really quick that underneath the suave smile and slick words that lured me in, was a darkness I had yet to experience in this lifetime. I entered a world filled with darkness, lies, brutality and extreme emotional pain. The physical bruises went away quickly, but it was the daily verbal destruction that took years to rid myself of; some of it still lingers in the deep recesses of my mind and if I am not careful, I can find myself still trapped in those lies. Due to the nature of my circumstances and that the very real threat to my life still remains, I cannot divulge much of what exactly I endured except that I lived with a shovel on my deck as a daily reminder of what I would be buried with. There was a constant threat of being sold into human trafficking or disappearing just like all the women on the "Highway of Tears" in British Columbia. This threat I took very seriously because a friend of mine who owed some of his acquaintances some money, was taken and put in a motel room for a month in Chetwynd, BC and made to pay it back in the form of sex for $40 at a time. Her boyfriend was made to stay in the room next to her to listen to her being beaten and repeatedly raped. I saw her once after her ordeal; she was never the same person I knew and ended up disappearing never to be seen again. I was terrified my fate would be similar even though I didn't owe anyone any money, a threat of this kind makes a person walk on eggshells. I tried to escape his clutches, but no matter where I went he would find me and force me back. He would constantly break into my house and write messages of brutality on my walls. He would have his people watch my every move and tell me exactly what I had done during the day. When I was able to find refuge, he would somehow find me and threaten the lives of all who resided in the house, as well as list off the addresses of their immediate families with names and places of work. He would come up close to them and take a Polaroid picture, and laugh like crazy saying this would be the last smiling face they ever saw! He truly was a psychopath and he wasn't about to let me go easily. I was constantly in and out of women's shelters while still working at the hospital. I was trying to save money so I could somehow escape him, but never seemed able to do so.

It was 2005 when I finally had to send my daughter to go live with her dad as her safety was in jeopardy. I had gone to the local store after my daughter was in bed to go get a small bottle of vodka, and when I came back he was waiting for me in the doorway. I was bent over untying my boots and looked over at him wondering why in the world was he holding a screwdriver? As I stood up, he came out of the shadows and hit me so hard in the face that I flew back 2 feet into the wall. He then threw an 8-inch long army bayonet knife that he owned from when he was in the Special Forces in the army. He missed me on purpose by a half an inch and told me I had exactly 2 minutes to get out of the house or he was going to kill both me and my daughter. We lived up in Whitehorse, Yukon at the time and in the middle of winter, cabs don't come quickly. God was with me because when I called the cab company, they said there just happened to be one outside my door! Unbelievable! Off the women's shelter I went where I spent 3 days awake, throwing up at the very idea of having to send my girl to live with her dad. It was then that she made me a card with a golden Inuksuk surrounded by gold stars, which I have to this day. It says," Hey Mom! I respect your decision and I won't be mad at you. Do what's right for you and I trust you will make the right decision. I love you, mom." What 10-year-old kid says that? The hardest part of sending her to safety was the fact that I would be left wide open to disappearing in the vastness of the Yukon where no-one would ever find me, then she would be left without a mother. I decided I just absolutely had to send her to her dad's for her own safety, while I planned and prayed how I would get out of my situation alive. This has been by far the most difficult decision I have ever had to make. He had a "friend" of dangerous nature that came to live with us who would follow my every move and report back to him. I was under constant surveillance and the stress was unbearable. I had to pretend that everything was fine at work while planning to escape my nightmare in one piece and not in several parts thrown to the wolves in the northern parts of the Yukon or Northwest Territories.

The day when I put my daughter on the bus to go meet her dad was by far the hardest day of my life. My world completely collapsed after from this day forth. I simply had lost all will to live and plowed through complete darkness for the next year unable to get out of my situation for fear of my life. I just could not seem to get back on track and the situation worsened every single minute that went by. I had several dreams during this period that helped me see what I needed to do next; I discuss these in the following chapter. The Spiritual component to them is incredibly powerful so I am dedicating a whole chapter to this very important aspect of my life.

The final straw came one day as I arrived home from work. For no particular reason, I must've looked at him wrong, as I turned to go to the bathroom, he moved 20 feet in literally the blink of an eye and was upon me in seconds. All I had time to do was turn away from him to face the bathroom, and he was on me like a bolt of lightning. He threw me on the floor and was sitting on my chest covering both my arms with his legs. He began strangling me hard with one hand while punching me in the face with the other. I couldn't breathe and was beginning to lose consciousness and saw only giant gold stars in my vision. He was screaming at me so hard that veins were popping and his face was red like a tomato. It's interesting the things you notice when you think it is the end of your life. Time seemed to trickle as I could see his carotid artery pump blood and wondered about mine stopping. I could see the spit goblets come flying out of his mouth as he screamed at me inches away from my face, his vein throbbing at his temple amidst the starry vision I had. Everything seemed to happen in slow motion as I dimly heard him scream," I am going to take your bloodied, battered body, tie you up, put you in a truck, roll you down a hill and burn you alive you stupid, useless bitch! DO YOU DOUBT ME?" By this time, his words were fading out and I was losing consciousness and could no longer move or think as I welcomed the blackness that was surrounding me from all directions. It was all I could do to barely shake my head. I felt hot tears slide down my cheeks as I gratefully embraced the darkness around me. He suddenly released the pressure on my neck and grabbed me by the hair and dragged me up the stairs and locked me in the room. As I lay on the bed struggling to regain my breath, I heard him leave the house, fiddle with my car and drive away in my other vehicle. I knew instinctively this was my one and only chance at living...if I didn't get the heck out now, I knew this was going to be the beginning of the end for me. Although my face was throbbing, and my head was incredibly fuzzy trying to put my thoughts in order, survival kicked in and I called a friend in Edmonton to buy me a one-way bus ticket to Edmonton. My voice was barely recognizable due to the strangling and my friend had a difficult time believing what I was telling him, but helped me anyway thankfully. Little did he know that he just saved my life for real. God Bless his kind Soul.

In Whitehorse, there is only one bus a day that heads south and I only had an hour to make it there. I knew if I didn't escape now, I would be dead in the very near future and no one would ever find me. I broke down the bedroom door, threw some clothes in a bag and tried to take my car, but he had disabled it so I couldn't leave. He had also taken my bank card with him so I had absolutely no money either. I ended up making it to the bus with exactly 2 minutes to spare. As I sat down and breathed a sigh of relief that my friend had actually come through with the ticket, I saw him driving slowly by the bus looking intently into the windows. He must've returned home and found me gone and came looking for me. Luckily for me the bus was already moving and he couldn't do a darn thing about it. The whole scene was like out of a movie and seemed to happen in slow motion. I had completely stopped breathing as I saw his car creep by and realized I had slid down into the bottom of the seat hoping and praying to God that he didn't see me. Fresh, hot tears were streaming down my face as I thanked God for the bus driving away leaving him behind. I cried all the way to Watson Lake, which is a 5-hour drive, where I made a phone call to the restaurant in Edmonton I would work at periodically during the busy seasons. The boss loved me and gladly hired me back on the spot and told me to show up for work as soon as I was settled in 2 days. I then called my good friend Don who has always kept a basement apartment just for me and my complicated life crises. Thank God for Don and his everlasting faith in me! He said he would have it ready for me when I arrived within the next couple of days as the bus ride was 36 hours long.

This is how I have spent my entire life living. Regardless of the situation at hand, in times of survival, I will do whatever it takes to live. In this case, I needed a job desperately as well as a place to stay so I made a few calls and wham! I was set! In this very critical moment however, I immediately stored and put away the last 7 years of trauma in a locked box in the deep recesses of my mind...hopefully never to be dealt with again. Accompanied with the violence, I had endured 2 miscarriages, and was strangled to the point of losing consciousness 3 separate times, plus countless other death threats. However, I chose to pretend it never happened. For now though, I was facing a possible future with at least a job and roof over my head, so why even bother with what happened in the past? Let it stay where it belonged...in the past! I was making a new beginning for myself and I was safe for the time being. I prayed and prayed to God that this time he would leave me alone and find someone else to torment. He had broken into this very apartment where I was going before, so the fear that he would show up was very real but I had nowhere else to go for the time being. The plan was to stay there and save money until I could get another place in a different area of the city closer to my daughter.

Many people in life make the same mistake I did by choosing to leave the past in the past. I had to discover the hard way that by not addressing the past issues only made my life more complicated and difficult to manage. You don't have to live in the past, but at least go face the trauma of it so you will be able to let it go and be free from it. Otherwise, it will become excess baggage you carry with you everywhere you go and gets harder to get rid of.

When it comes to abusive relationships, many people do not understand the invisible barrier that keeps the victim frozen in place for so long. They ask," Why don't they just leave?" It's not that simple. When there are children involved it is especially difficult due to the immediate threat on their lives. The danger is very real and the victim becomes the puppet doing whatever the puppet master wants when he pulls the strings attached. In my case, the stalking, the constant death threats and the violence all around me kept me in a place where I could barely function. I felt I could not go the police because of who he was and the kind of people he was involved with; I would most definitely disappear before I had a chance to do anything legally. Did I look constantly over my shoulder? Absolutely! I was terrified and constantly afraid that he would just randomly show up...but he never did. He must've found some other poor Soul to control because from that moment on, he left me alone. I don't understand why or how, but I really don't care...as long as he leaves me alone. Thank you, God! He kept both my cars, all my household furniture and every single thing I owned, but I truly didn't care as I was alive and had a yet another chance at starting over. Little did I realize that there was no more room in my head to continue to pretend as if nothing happened. I was done and would soon have to face the biggest demon yet – myself!

Boundaries are by far the best thing I could have ever learned in life. Recognizing your boundaries will help you define appropriate behaviour for yourself and those around you. You will be better able to determine your role in a relationship because you will know your limits. It helps in not allowing others to define who you are – that is *yours* to decide! Your self-worth is NOT determined by what someone else says it is! It is what YOU say it is! What do YOU think of you? I didn't know that - I really didn't and that is so very sad.

How does one learn to develop healthy boundaries?[8]

- Pay attention to your feelings – they provide *you* with valuable information.
- Find out for yourself what *you* like, need and want – what do *you* desire; not what someone else wants from you. Getting to know yourself helps with knowing your boundaries and learning to set them.
- List what makes *you* unique and different – value yourself and know your limits.
- How *you* are willing to allow yourself to be treated by yourself and others.
- Don't forget that what you tolerate is what will continue; good or bad.

When we know we need to set a limit with someone, do it clearly and in a few words as possible: avoid justifying, rationalizing or apologizing. This was very, very hard to do and I still struggle with it. The most important person to notify of our boundary is "ourselves". Remember that you cannot set a boundary and worry about the other person's feelings. That is their problem to deal with – *not yours!* You also have

---

to recognize that where there were previously no boundaries that were set, and all of a sudden there is one, this may bring feelings of anger and resentment from the other person. Tell yourself, "So what?" Be prepared to follow through with your actions and behaviour as they need to match the set boundary. Boundaries are a personal issue and reflect and contribute to our growth, ourselves, our connection to ourselves and to others. Boundaries are set to take care of ourselves, not to control others. YOU are number one in YOUR life! Don't ever forget that!

I have listed some codependent behaviours below that are found in the book "Codependent No More" by Melody Beattie. Check off the ones you can relate to. For more information, "The Language of Letting Go" is also a good daily meditation by Melody Beattie.

- My good feelings about who I am stem from being liked and approved by *you*.
- *Your* struggles affect my peace of mind.
- My mental attention focuses on solving *your* problems or reliving *your* pain.
- My main goal is to please *you*.
- My attention is on protecting *you*.
- My self-esteem is bolstered by solving *your* problem.
- My own hobbies and interests are put aside. My time is spent sharing *your* interests and hobbies.
- The dreams I have for my future are linked to *you*.
- My fear of *your* rejection determines what I say or do.
- My fear of *your* anger determines what I say or do.
- I use giving as a way of feeling safe in our relationship.
- My social circle diminishes as I involve myself with *you*.
- I value *your* opinion and way of doing things more than my own.

- The quality of my life is in relation to the quality of *yours*.
- I am not aware of how I feel. I am aware of how *you* feel.
- I am not aware of what I want. I ask what *you* want.

If you have checked off more than 3 of these, I really suggest you read "Codependent No More" and educate yourself on Boundaries and Codependency. It just might change your life, because it sure did for me. It is about learning who *you* are and what *you* will tolerate in your life. There are many various free worksheets on the internet today to help you to figure out where you stand with your own personal boundaries. The word YOU is underlined because of the importance of the word. Think about how often this word is used in your vocabulary?

Here is a quote from the book "Codependent No More":

> "All of me, every aspect of my being, is important. I count for something. I matter. My feelings can be trusted. My thinking is appropriate. I value my wants and needs. I do not deserve and will not tolerate abuse or constant mistreatment. I have rights, and it is my responsibility to assert these rights. The decisions I make and the way I conduct myself will reflect my high self-esteem. My decisions will take into account my responsibilities to myself."
>
> Melody Beattie

Here are some statistics taken from the Canadian Women's Foundation:

→ Approximately every six days, a woman in Canada is killed by her intimate partner. Out of the 83 police-reported intimate partner homicides in 2014, 67 of the victims—over 80%—were women.

→ On any given night in Canada, 3,491 women and their 2,724 children sleep in shelters to escape abuse; about 300 women and children are turned away because shelters are already full.

→ There were 1,181 cases of missing or murdered Aboriginal women in Canada between 1980 and 2012, according to the RCMP. However, according to grassroots organizations and the Minister of the Status of Women, the number is much higher, closer to 4,000.

→ Aboriginal women are killed at six times the rate of non-aboriginal women.

→ 7 in 10 people who experience family violence are women and girls.

→ Women are about four times as likely as men to be victims of intimate partner homicide.

→ Women often stay because the abuser has threatened to kill them if they leave, or to kill himself, or to kill the children. Women believe these threats for good reason—the most dangerous time for an abused woman is when she attempts to leave her abuser.

→ About 26% of all women who are murdered by their spouse had left the relationship. In one study, half of the murdered women were killed within two months of leaving the relationship.

→ Women are 6 times more likely to be killed by an ex-partner than by a current partner. Many women say that they were abused by a partner after the relationship ended, and that the violence escalated following a break-up.

→ Almost 60% of all dating violence happens after the relationship has ended.

➤ Some women stay because the abuser has threatened to harm or kill a household pet. In one study, 57% of survivors of domestic violence had their pet killed by an abusive partner.

➤ Women might stay because they are financially dependent on their partner; leaving an abusive relationship may involve a choice between violence and poverty and nowhere to go. The mental health consequences of abuse can make it difficult for women to leave a relationship. 64% of battered women exhibit symptoms of post-traumatic stress disorder (PTSD).

➤ Rates of violence against women vary widely across Canada. As is the case with violent crime overall, the territories have consistently recorded the highest rates of police-reported violence against women. The rate of violent crime against women in Nunavut in 2011 was nearly 13 times higher than the rate for Canada. Saskatchewan and Manitoba, which have consistently recorded the highest provincial rates of police-reported violent crime, had rates of violence against women in 2011 that were about double the national rate. Ontario and Quebec had the lowest rates of violence against women.

Types of Abuse

➤ Physical abuse: Slapping, hitting or strangulation as a demonstration of power and control. Using hands or objects as weapons. Threatening her with a knife or gun. Committing murder.

➤ Sexual abuse: Using threats, intimidation, or physical strength to force her into unwanted sexual acts.

➤ Emotional or verbal abuse: Threatening to kill her (or to kill the children, other family members or pets), threatening to commit suicide, making humiliating or degrading comments about her body or behaviour, forcing her to commit degrading acts, isolating her from friends or family, confining her to the house, destroying her possessions, and other actions designed to demean her or to restrict her freedom and independence.

→ Financial abuse: Stealing or controlling her money or valuables (of particular concern to older women). Forcing her to work. Denying her the right to work.

→ Spiritual abuse: Using her religious or spiritual beliefs to manipulate, dominate, and control her.

→ Criminal harassment/stalking: Following her or watching her in a persistent, malicious, and unwanted manner. Invading her privacy in a way that threatens her personal safety.

If you are experiencing ANY form of abuse, start asking yourself the hard questions about why you are in this relationship to begin with and why would you tolerate any form of mistreatment? The longer you tolerate it, the more it will happen. Recognize that domestic abuse is often a gradual process, with the frequency of assaults and seriousness of the violence slowly escalating over time. Watch for any signs or "red flags" that show up. Pay attention to the little things and change in behaviours. Address the issue as soon as it arises because the longer it takes for you to do something about it, the harder it becomes to leave. Since abusers often express deep remorse and promise to change, it can take years for women to admit that the violence will never stop and the relationship cannot be fixed. The long-term experience of being abused can destroy a woman's self-confidence and self-worth, making it more difficult for her to believe that she deserves better treatment, that she can find the courage to leave, or that she can manage on her own.[9] I know this because I lived it most of my life, from my mother's

---

9   Canadian Women's Foundation

experience with my crazy step-father to the abusive relationships I endured for years. People assume that you can just leave; there's a lot more to the story than that. Life becomes a vicious cycle and increasingly hard, but if you are currently experiencing this type of existence, *do something* to help yourself get out. There are resources available – go find them. Only YOU can take a step in the right direction – trust your instincts! It took me 7 years of hell to finally get the courage to leave and change my life. Know in your heart that it is possible. It is far from easy and the first months will be the hardest to get through, but you will get through it. One step at a time; one day at a time. As long as you tolerate the abuse, it will only get worse. Find the courage to make that change for yourself and if you have children, for them as well. You might not see the end of it right now, but there truly is a light at the end of the tunnel. Find the strength to keep putting one foot in front of the other and stay away from the abuser as best as you can. Even though you may not believe it, you carry deep within you the power to get up and leave. You are stronger than you think. You are braver than you think.

"Courage is not living without fear; Courage is being scared to death and doing the right thing anyway."

~Chae Richardson~

STOP AND REFLECT:

1. Have you ever experienced any type of abuse? If yes, which one: Mental, Physical, Verbal, Sexual, Financial or Spiritual?

_____

_____

_____

_____

_____

2. When re-evaluating your current situation, ask yourself: are there any red flags that I missed? Any signs or warnings that the abuse was pending such as demeaning comments or remarks? Outbursts of rage that were over the top? Any name calling, pushing or shoving? Hands around your throat? Isolating you from your friends and family? Remember that abuse starts small and gradually grows.

_____

_____

_____

_____

_____

_____

3. If you are currently experiencing any form of abuse, take a long, hard look at your life and determine the next steps you need to take to leave the situation at hand.

_____

_____

_____

_____

_____

_____

4. What resources are in your area that will assist you in times of distress? It is good practice to have these numbers on hand and have a plan of escape. What is your plan to remaining safe?

_____

_____

_____

_____

_____

_____

KATHY
AS LONG
AS YOU
DRINK
ALCOHOL
YOU WILL
NOT
HAVE
ACCESS
TO THIS BOO

Chapter 7:

DEMONS & DREAMS

DREAMS:

Dreams are a series of images, ideas, emotions, and sensations occurring involuntarily in the mind during certain stages of sleep.[10]

The topic of dreams is a widely discussed subject with much speculation and difference of opinions. In my personal life, dreams have played a constant role and very real aspect of guiding me in all areas of my life. Since they vividly began with the dream of Jesus that I mentioned in Chapter 2, they have been a part of my story and have been such a blessing. I have learned to interpret them in ways that only I would understand, because really, who else is better suited than the dreamer himself to be able to understand the meaning? Obtaining it out of a book on dreams is a generalized and fictitious manner, not to mention someone else's opinion. How can someone else possibly tell me what my dream means? That never made sense to me. Every dream is given to the dreamer for them to decipher the meaning. It's a personalised connection meant to help you figure out problems in your own world. If you learn to pay close attention to your dreams, you will quickly recognize the connection with your everyday life. It

10   www.thefreedictionary.com/dream

all starts with having a dream journal. I have been writing down my dreams since 1985; it's too bad that I lost that book when I left all my belongings in Whitehorse. My greatest loss in material belongings was that book because some of the dreams I have had over the years were just like in the movies. Unbelievable at best! The other worlds that I have travelled to many, many times; the places and the people I have met on the other side have been of a spiritual nature that doesn't exist here on earth. Dreams truly are the forgotten portal into the heavenly kingdom; they are a pathway into the other worlds which are only separated by a very fine invisible line. As soon as you fall asleep, you automatically cross over to the other side and can explore the vast universe at will. You can learn so much from your dream experiences if you pay attention and put in a little effort before you fall asleep by putting your attention on the third eye (the area in between your eyes). As you take deep breaths, sing a mantra of yours or try the word HU, fill yourself with all the love that you have, and put your focus on the blank screen inside your mind. You can create any image you wish of where you would like to be. Hear the sounds, feel the experience, smell the scents...use your imagination to create a place where you can explore to your liking. Before you know it, you will be there living the experience. If you do this for 10- 20 minutes every night, you start to see a difference in the quality of your dreams as well as your waking life. You can get to a point where you can control what happens in the dream – like when I was taught to make myself invisible when in danger. Your dreams will guide you in your life if you can learn to interpret them.

I had a dream once regarding the illusions we face in life. I was in another era located in a tiny village somewhere in Scotland and was a commoner woman in a village that didn't have much of anything really. A man on a wooden chariot type wagon with 4 black huge, grand and majestic horses pulling it came into view. The man in the chariot resembled an Ancient Greek God in his sheer beauty...an ADONIS! His hair was long and golden with waves flowing around his broad shoulders. He stood at least 6 foot 4 inches tall and his muscular, tanned body glistened with a moisture from the heat of the night. His wide spaced eyes were a deep blue like I had never seen before thus completely hypnotizing me and instantly putting me under his spell. The raw power and almost superhuman strength exuded from all pores of his golden skin. The brawniness of the bronzed muscles was a sight to behold indeed leaving me breathless just to look at him. I was entranced as he approached me with the wagon and slowed down to a stop. He smiled a perfect smile that made my stomach flutter like butterflies in a flower field. I was completely hypnotized by his angelic beauty and would have followed him to the ends of the earth had he asked me. He knew the power he held over me because he ever so graciously held out his hand and asked that I accompany him for a ride. Without skipping a beat, I accepted and got in the chariot beside this beauty of a man almost swooning with giddiness to be so close to him. He took me out of town to an opening in the woods where we both stepped down to the grassy field. As I gazed at him completely taken by his incredible beauty, his perfectly chiseled face suddenly turned into the snarling face of a lion! The transformation took me by complete surprise as did the aggressiveness of the pending attack. His teeth became fangs and he had a long, slimy tongue that spit out a venom meant to kill me. His legs transformed into hind legs with paws, and his arms became powerful front legs with claws meant to shred me into a thousand pieces. This angel-turned-beast began to prance around me in a fashion due to a boxer; jumping from one hind paw to the other. His front claws would attempt to rip at me, but for some reason, I was surrounded by an invisible energy that evil could not touch. This made the beast all the angrier, so it began to hiss and spit fire as it pranced furiously around me attempting to shred me to pieces. I felt absolutely no fear as I watched this beast move effortlessly around me. I knew I had a Spiritual Protection around me that no evil could ever touch, so all I did was wait and watch him go. Quite frankly, it was a tad amusing to me watching him get angrier and angrier at his inability to attack and kill me.

→ This dream taught me to not believe in what is on the outside because the inside could be a nasty demon waiting to come out. It will hide behind beauty, sultry smiles, and slick moves… beware and pay attention to what lies beneath it was the ultimate meaning of the dream. Beauty needs to come from within and not just what physical appearances are. Really pay attention to people around you and look for what lies deep inside, then you will see the beauty radiate outwards. This dream really did change my perspective on the way I looked at people. I look beneath the physical aspect and search for the darkness lying beneath the smiles. I am always aware of the possibilities of what lies beneath.

The following 4 dreams came to me while I was going through that incredibly difficult time up in Whitehorse, Yukon. I believe they were given to me to help me understand the next step I needed to take in life.

i. I dreamt I woke up to a giant Book of Light the size of the house wall. It was magnificent in its splendor and brightness, completely hypnotizing me as I approached it wanting only more of this bright, white light. As if in a trance, I walked towards it in complete awe, but as I approached it, the book slammed shut in my face! I couldn't believe it and was completely devastated! I backed up and the book opened up a second time so I approached it tentatively. As I got closer, it slammed shut again! Now I was confounded and a tad hurt by this rebuttal! Why was it doing this? This is my only link to God so why am I not allowed to get close? Suddenly the book opened up a third time, but giant words began popping randomly out of the Light. My name came first and the words were being read aloud by a booming, deep voice. It said: "Kathy - As long as you drink alcohol you will not have access to this book!" It proceeded to slam shut so hard that I literally fell out of my bed waking up from the dream! I was so devastated by this message because I felt rejected by God Himself. Didn't He understand my situation? The abandonment was overwhelming and I cried for 3 days straight as the realization sank in. I came to the conclusion that my connection to that Light was far more important than any bottle could ever be. I vowed to quit the alcohol intake as soon as I got out of my mess that I was currently living and pursue that Book of Light instead.

Clearly, the meaning of this dream was to quit drinking alcohol if I wanted to progress on the Spiritual Path that I so desperately wanted. This very vivid dream has been at the forefront of all my relapses in my battles with alcohol. The Book of Light is everything to me, but the clutches of addiction were powerful and the negative was holding me prisoner steadfastly. This remained a daily reminder of what I was working towards.

ii.   In this dream, I was walking around downtown Whitehorse carrying with me all the luggage I had. I was burdened down with so much extra weight from the baggage that I could barely walk. I struggled with each and every step of the way as the extra weight became unbearable. I had bags tied around my head; a backpack overloaded with stuff coming out the seams; baggage tied around my waist and some on each hip; there was luggage tied to other luggage that I was dragging around with me everywhere I went. Neither the banks, restaurants nor any stores would let me in with all that excess baggage, which left me stranded on the street wondering what to do. Along came this giant beast of a woman the size of a football player, so I smiled happily and asked her to kindly help me carry this around. She jumped back as if I had the plaque and put her hands up in protest with fear in her eyes. She said: "No Way Man! I am NOT touching that load! You have to deal with THAT on your own!" With that being said, she backed away from me slowly as if I had a gun pointed at her leaving me confused as to why no one would let me in or even want to help me carry the load. I awoke standing on the street corner with nothing but my luggage holding me back and nowhere to go with it.

This dream was very obvious to me: I would not advance any further in this life until I got rid of all the excess baggage I was carrying around with me everywhere I went. This baggage was all the trauma, pain, neglect and abuse I had endured for a lifetime without ever dealing with it. It is impossible to go through so much and not have help with it at a therapeutic level. The dream was clear: You need to let it go and you won't take another step in any direction until you do. It is not up to other people to deal with what was handed to you in this lifetime. It is mine and mine alone to deal with it and get the necessary help I needed. I have a quote with a picture of a beautiful butterfly attempting to fly up a set of steep stairs while carrying a giant rock attached to its body by a thick string. The quote says, "Let Shit Go!" This represents me and what I used to be like. A fragile person trying to carry a world of weight on her shoulders on a journey that is all uphill. I believe that a good portion of the population of today is similar; we go about life carrying a heavy load of "Crap" which makes every single step seem uphill. It doesn't need to be this way.

iii. I was being chased by my crazy boyfriend with a butcher knife trying to kill me. I was knee deep in snow so running from him was very difficult and I wasn't getting anywhere fast. He was gaining ground and catching up with me fast. Terrified, I look up and see a new, big, black truck running and it was as if it was waiting for me to get in. I jumped in and turned to see where he was, but the truck had an energy force just like in Star Wars so he couldn't come close to me whatsoever, which only infuriated him more. I looked straight ahead and see a very steep hill made of sheer ice and full of ice blocks making going up this hill almost impossible. I felt defeated leaving one mess and jumping right into another one. Before I could even stop to gain my thoughts, the truck began driving by itself without my hands being even on the wheel! How is that possible? The truck maneuvered itself just fine avoiding all the ice blocks, and made its way slowly up the hill. Feeling panicky about letting the truck drive itself, I grabbed onto the steering wheel to try and control the truck, but the second I did that, down the hill I went backwards to where I had originally started. I thought to myself, "What is up with that?" and let go of the wheel. Before I could even answer my own question, the truck went up the hill again on its own without my help. This time, I was able to let it do its thing until almost the top, then my lack of Faith made me instinctively put my hands on the wheel again. Guess what happened? Yep! Down the hill I went, all the way to the bottom where I had started twice before! Really? I sat there contemplating my situation, when the truck started making its way through the ice blocks and steep hill for the third time. I finally clued in (geez...I'm a little slow) and figured out that maybe I should just have some Faith and let the truck do its thing without my assistance. Sure enough, the truck made its way to the top of the steep incline and onto a 5-lane busy highway and drove itself through all the traffic with no problem – and without my assistance either!

This dream was pretty easy for me to understand; just like the song says, "Let Jesus Take the Wheel!" When life is seemingly all uphill, try to have some Faith that the Universe will guide you where you need to be and watch out for the roadblocks in front of you. Every time I tried to take the wheel away from the Force that was guiding the truck; down the hill I went. The minute I trusted enough in God or the Universe, the truck was able to make its way where it needed to be. Have Faith! I refer to this dream regularly in my daily life when I get frustrated with things when they aren't going my way. I just stop and think about this very dream and take my hands off the wheel of the problem that is plaguing me, and let God take over. It always ends up with a better result anyway!

iv. This last one happened right before I sent Tanis to her father's for her safety. This dream showed me exactly who and what I was up against. I dreamt that I was accompanied by a Spiritual Guide floating above the room where there was a party going on with all my boyfriend's associates. I could see every member sitting around that table (about 20) all of whom were attached by a cord that was being directed by a Puppet Master who was a dark, and very evil Entity of the Devil. This Entity owned every member around the table as well as around the world, and controlled them all in the same way; thus giving them the feeling of a deep brotherhood bond. This is accurate as the connection they had in real life was exactly that...a brotherhood of the same family; almost blood brothers you could say. They dress, think and behave all in the same way and even look alike! I understood many things as I watched them sit around all unaware of the invisible lines attaching them to this Entity above who guided their every action, thought and deeds.

All of a sudden, the ground shook as if the rumblings of an earthquake was making its way towards us. The earth began to crack and open up into wide canyons revealing the red fires of hell extending into infinity beneath the floor. The men sitting at the table cowered and winced with fear as they knew who and what was approaching them menacingly. I felt only sheer curiosity and actually craned my neck to get a better view of what was approaching us with such force. We remained invisible and were only acting as bystanders watching the scene play out as if it were a movie being filmed.

Curiously, I looked to see what was slowly stomping its way towards us, and to my utter surprise, there was my boyfriend at the time making his way towards us. However, he was the size of a giant with lizard type eyes that spat out deadly red laser rays that would instantly disintegrate everything in its path. This beast was searching for someone (me) that it knew was around but just couldn't see. This is because I was under the Spiritual Protection of the Guide that was with me whose job was to protect me at all costs. The creature smelled and searched for me knowing I was close but unable to detect my whereabouts. It reminded me of the movie "Aliens" and I watched with complete awe and surprisingly no fear whatsoever. This creature had complete and utter control over all the puppets (members) and their entity in the room below it. The scene fascinated me as I continued to watch it continue to search and slowly make its way along getting further and further from me. I thanked my guide for the understanding of this experience and woke up.

This dream showed me exactly what and whom I was up against in the man I called my boyfriend. I knew that I had to be extremely careful in my approach and dealings with him and had a clear understanding of the danger I was in. I now knew why he was seemingly able to find me anywhere I would try to hide when attempting to escape him. He knowingly has a nasty entity hanging around him guiding him and controlling his every thought, action, and deed in this life. Just like his so called "brothers." This dream confirmed what I already knew to be true.

It's interesting to note here that after this dream, I decided to go to a Shaman (a tribal healer who can act as a medium between the visible and spirit world) in Whitehorse for assistance on the matter. My boyfriend insisted on coming with me (more for making sure I was where I said I would be). The Shaman did a session for the both of us and in my case, she said that I had a zoo of entities that were surrounding me and that the number of entities surrounding me had never been witnessed before. She was in shock and took quite some time at ridding me of them, even mentioning to me that I would be off balance for a few days afterward. She was right because I was falling over everywhere as if I was intoxicated, dropping things and completely off balance for the next 2 days after the visit.

She explained they most likely came when we played with the Ouija Board when we were teenagers. She said we opened up an invisible portal to them who come to people through the use of drugs and alcohol. They can easily take over your body when you are under the influence thus explaining the "blackouts" when your mind is gone but your body is still functioning. Very dangerous indeed! She said they "hang around" people with addictions because they feed off the energy they project and can easily take over a human body if it is not protected.

When it came to my boyfriend, she was even more surprised because she said his entity was so huge and all-consuming that there was no possible way to do it by herself and that she would need the help of 2 or 3 other Shamans! She had never seen anything so evil and of that magnitude living in one person. She had tried a few different things to attack it, but was quickly rebutted and tossed her aside, thus being unable to approach this thing inside him. She was at a loss and looked at me to tell me to be very careful with him because of what was lurking beneath. I told her "I know...I saw It in a dream" He just laughed at her because he has always known he had a "buddy" lurking around with him and quite frankly, he loved it. The power it gave him heightened his senses and fed his already large ego. He was a legend in his own mind so her comment only fueled his ego...great, just what I needed.

Here is one last dream for you to understand the connection between the dream worlds and our lives. In this dream, I was walking down a brand new paved road that led straight into the horizon. As I walked, I split into 2 separate people: the old Kathy and the new Kathy. The old version of me was sidetracked by all these big, beautiful and sparkly wrapped gift boxes with giant colorful bows on the top, which were on the side of the road and she couldn't focus on the path she needed to walk down. She was all over the place running excitedly back and forth from one present to the next. She was completely unaware there was even a new road that she should be walking on that led to happiness, because she was so very distracted by bright new and shiny things. She was muttering to herself and talking rapidly as she ran back and forth, and quite frankly appeared very unstable and borderline crazy. She was really annoying this new me who only wanted to walk the straight and narrow road that led into the sunset.

I had no desire for the gifts so I wasn't distracted in the least, and just kept walking regardless of the old version cutting me off and trying to distract me from my goal. I looked sadly at her run around, and thought to myself; "She will never get anywhere as long as she is distracted by everything that comes her way." The more I looked at her, the more I wanted to be far away from her negativity and seemingly lost Soul. She was walking behind me at one point then pushed me out of the way so she could pass me in an effort to get to another gift further up the road. She had no cares for the journey itself, only what was being given to her. She said to me: "I don't want to be with you anymore because you are too fat and walk too slow. You are in my way so I am leaving you behind." With that, she quickly walked ahead of me muttering to herself about something and went straight to a giant box on the side of the road that had a big bow on it. She stopped right there and didn't move again. I walked by her and looked sadly at her, thinking to myself; "I am sad to leave her behind in such a state, but am glad to be rid of her so I can continue on my path to happiness."

This dream had a deep meaning: letting go of the old self with the old belief system, and grasp onto a new and stronger version of myself. If you want to advance in life, you have to be willing to let go of old ideas that weren't working for you and try new ones. We are our own biggest obstacles in life; we often stop ourselves from advancing due to insecurity and low self-esteem. This dream stayed with me because I could take a long, hard look at what I was like and what I needed to change. Who did I want to be like: the old version who fluttered everywhere with no real destination and full of distractions? Or the new one who took slow, steady steps in the right direction regardless of what came her way?

Dreams are very powerful and most often prophetic if you can learn to decipher them. The mind acts like a filter making the true meaning a mess most times. If you can learn to pick them apart, you will see just how they really do relate to your everyday life. It needs to start with a Dream Journal and the self-discipline to write them down as soon as you wake up, even if it's in the middle of the night. If you do not work at this discipline, the dream will be gone in seconds and you will have lost it. I suggest you keep a specific book just to write your dreams by your bedside; you can always type them up later and keep a dream file on your computer. I hand write them every single time because I get a better feel for them when it comes from hand to paper. This might not work for you. Do what works best for your lifestyle, even its notes from specific points from the dream and then go back later. However, I have found when I did this, I would still forget important parts of the dream that could later be useful in determining the underlying meaning. It never ceases to amaze me at just how fast they disappear, even sometimes while I am writing them, off they go into the fog.

When I go back and look at the dates I had a specific dream and I re-read what I had dreamt, often the two are directly related. I can usually see how the dream was actually telling me something was about to happen in the coming future. A good example of was almost every single time I would have extreme difficulties in life, I would dream that I would be surrounded by 7-8 nasty tornadoes; or I would be swimming and 100 foot waves would be coming my way; or be stuck in the mud up to my waist or even sometimes my neck! Sometimes I would be waist deep in thick and heavy snow and have difficulties taking a next step. After a dream of this type, I knew something difficult to overcome was coming so I would pay attention and at least was forewarned. Dreams touch every level of our life. They may let us glimpse the far away past, the future, give suggestions for healing, or share insights into our relationships.

I would like to touch on nightmares as I am pretty sure every single person alive has had the nasty experience of a nightmare that was so real, you believed it to be true. Since we played the Ouija board when I was 13, some of my dreams had become nightmares and it's as if we opened up a portal for them to haunt us continually. I was plagued by demons appearing at night while I was sleeping. The first time it happened, I was sleeping when I awoke (I thought I was awake) to a high powered wind (tornado type) in my room. Everything in the room was being swept into the depths of the whirlwind tempest above my bed. A giant black entity grabbed a hold of my feet and wrapped me in my blankets in a spinning motion. This very powerful thing was lifting me off the bed and flipping me upside down and smashing me into the bed. It lifted me up and flung me around only to throw me on the bed once again. All my books, papers, clothing, teddy bears, toys & trinkets were being tossed all around the room in a cyclone of wind that was only around my bed. I was so terrified of this negative being that I couldn't seem to find my voice to even cry out for help. As it gained force to throw me around harder, I suddenly thought to sing the powerful word my mom taught me the year before when I was struggling. I began to sing HU and the moment that powerful, yet loving word came out of my mouth, the wind stopped, the entity disappeared and I fell from the ceiling into my bed. Just like that, the whole experience just stopped with that one word. Unbelievable! I awoke with a feeling that I had just fallen into my bed, only to find my room as clean and everything in place like it was when I had gone to sleep a few hours before. I was so terrified of what has just occurred because it was so very, very real, that I fled to my mother's room screaming for her to wake up. Together we sang HU to bring peace and love back into the house. The experience was exactly like that seen in a movie! I literally could hear and feel the wind and the sounds of everything flying all over the place. The darkness of the entity that was holding my feet was very real to me. In my mind...it really happened and I was terrified to sleep in my room for the next while – always peeking to see if there was something there. It didn't come back for years to come thankfully. That being said, it did come back quite a few times over the years; especially when I was drinking as I was an easy portal of entry for them. They would show up constantly and I could very easily see them hanging around me. As soon as I would close my eyes, they were there attacking me. Sometimes, I would wake up with a sore stomach or arm where the entities would hit me. What did work for me was to throw blue balls of light at them; the spiritual power they held was no match for them so they would disappear. In some of the dreams, I would hear them speak an ancient language like the movie "The Mummy", their tongues long and poisonous in a snakelike shape. Terrifying to say the least! Since I have sobered up, I have had only one nasty entity come try to attack me during my sleep. I awoke with the feeling of its probing claws on my chest; so scary. Thank God it's over!

You might have many confusing dreams where the dream censor completely gives wrong cues as to what the real meaning is. It is up to you to write them down, no matter how strange they may seem, and try to figure out what the sub-conscious is trying to tell you. It can be like trying to put a puzzle together. I have had dreams where I can visit loved ones that have passed on and this has helped me tremendously with letting go once I see how happy they are. I have visited Spiritual Temples in other worlds with a beauty so intense that words simply cannot describe the beauty and energy coming from it. I have sat in classes learning about things that haven't been taught here yet; I had a private funeral for my grandmother when she passed on because I was unable to attend her funeral. She came to me in a classy, white suit and walked with me to her coffin in the church. I was able to have my closure as I spoke with her about the incredible worlds of the other side. My best friend and cousin whose funeral I was unable to attend, has come to me several times so I can see that she is happy where she is and tell me that all is right in the worlds of God. The last dream I had of her is when she came to tell me that she wouldn't be coming to see me again because she had to come back to earth now to fulfill her mission. Powerful to say the least!

Dreams will give you an understanding and an insight into other worlds that we cannot see with the naked eye. Your dreams are like a telescope that can give you a better view of something that is normally out of reach; your spiritual side. That includes how you act, feel, reflect, think, react, and even love. Most people fear putting the telescope of dreams to their eye, afraid of what they might see. Don't be afraid of the unknown; there are many wonderful worlds awaiting you.[11]

I learned to leave my body as a teenager and I have been flying free in my dreams since then, and I still do this today. Why walk when you can fly is my motto in the dream world! I was taught how to make myself invisible in times of danger in my dreams. The universe is a great place to explore and you have the freedom to do so in your dreams. I have had many dreams where I see past lives; I was a Roman Soldier who raped and killed women in the past; thus maybe explaining the rapes that occurred to me in this lifetime. One cannot escape the Law of Karma and every action has a consequence whether it be in this lifetime or the next. Our deeds will come back to haunt us at some point in time. I saw myself as a man being led up the stairs of the famous Roman Colosseum to his death from the ravishing claws of the lions. I could hear the screams of delight from the crowd as they were waiting to witness the bloody show. I saw myself as a young soldier being surrounded and killed in War World I. I saw myself as a woman jumping to her death in the river below from an old castle; thus possibly explaining my easily concluding that a jump from a bridge would be an easy way out. Dreams are a gift and very powerful tool if you can learn how to interpret them, and this really only can come from writing them down and finding the connection between the two worlds. If you do, it will give you an awareness that will help guide your footsteps as well as give you an understanding as to why certain things may happen to you in life. I have way too many dreams to list here, and the purpose is only to show you the Divine Connection that dreams have in your everyday life. Dreams have been the place

---

11   Beyond Meditation - Spiritual Experiences Guidebook

to go to since the beginning of mankind used by Kings, Pharaohs, prophets and disciples of Jesus.

Take your dreams into contemplation and you might have a pleasant surprise at what you see! Contemplation is a method that enables you to begin to actively explore the inner worlds of your own being. Give it a try 20 minutes every day, whether it be first thing in the morning before you start your day, or at night before you fall asleep. Sit in a quiet place and close your eyes thinking of someone you love or even a pet. Let that feeling of love into your heart center and put your attention on your inner third eye. It's a place between your eyebrows on the inner screen of your vision. You can imagine any scene you wish as this is your experience. You can imagine yourself walking a hilly valley with many beautiful flowers and feeling a warm breeze on your face. Imagine yourself lying down amidst the flowers as you watch the puffy, white clouds float by in the blue sky. Feel the inner peace and freedom as you lay there. You can imagine a passed loved one coming to sit with you to talk; you can imagine you are talking with an Angel or other Spiritual Figure you believe in; you can imagine you are soaring through the Universe flying within the stars; you can imagine putting all your current problems in a river of light so that the Universe will help you find a solution; you can be anywhere you want to be in your contemplation as this is your adventure. When you fall asleep, you might just be surprised as to what happens next in the dream world. Be sure to write it all down for future reference. This form of contemplation will help you in your daily life and give you an understanding on things that may be happening in your daily life. Be consistent with this and try to do it every day at the same time for a month so you can notice the difference in your daily life. You might just have a pleasant surprise!

"The future belongs to those who believe in the beauty of their dreams."

~Eleanor Roosevelt~

STOP & REFLECT:

1. Think about a recent dream that you may have had. What about it continues to trigger something inside you?

_____

_____

_____

_____

2. Have you ever had a dream where there is a bright, white light? Or even a dream with different colors? Or heard a sound that you can't quite explain? Write about it.

_____

_____

_____

_____

3. Think about a dream that you may have had with a loved one that has passed on. How did you feel afterwards? Even though you miss that person, did it help you when you awoke?

_____

_____

_____

_____

4. Have you ever had a dream that was so real you woke up believing
   it really happened? Do you believe in waking dreams? Déjà vu?
   Visions? Premonitions?

_____

_____

_____

_____

_____

Chapter 8

DARK NIGHT OF SOUL; CAN YOU GO ANOTHER ROUND?

Faith:

Faith is confidence or trust in a person or thing; or the observance of an obligation from loyalty; or fidelity to a person, promise, engagement; or a belief not based on proof; or it may refer to a particular system of religious belief, such as in which faith is confidence based on some degree of warrant. The term 'faith' has numerous connotations and is used in different ways, often depending on context. hopefulness · hopeantonyms: mistrustStrong belief in God or in the doctrines of a religion, based on spiritual apprehension rather than proof.[12]

Faith is what has kept me alive during the hardest times of my life. Even though my circumstances were quite extreme, I knew somewhere and somehow that something was going to change. I had faith that my situation was temporary and that I would pull myself out of the hell I was living. My dreams helped me understand where I was and what I needed to do to take the next step. Many times I would curse God and wonder why if He was such a loving God, how could all these

---

12   www.dictionary.com/browse/faith

bad things happen to me? However, deep down, I knew that if I was to pull through these conditions; I *needed to believe* that there was a power greater than myself taking care of me even if I didn't see the end result in sight. Although I didn't necessarily understand how I would get to where I needed to be, I trusted I would be shown the way and that my footsteps would be guided. The trick with Faith is that you have to be able to have the "Eyes to See" and the "Ears to Hear" what is being shown to you. You can be given all the gifts in the world, but if you don't learn to recognize what is on your path, then you can completely miss the lesson. Even though we don't understand what is going on in our lives, if we can learn how to pay attention to the signs given to us, then at least we have a guide to help us take another step in the right direction.

I kept looking to the sky to save me and was constantly looking for a sign of life, but at the end of the day it was ultimately up to me to take a step in the right direction first. I knew deep inside that I had an inner light that needed to burn bright, and I thought for sure someone or something would help me shine and do it for me. I had to learn that in order for the Universe to help me, I had to meet It halfway. I had to be the one to take that first step in surrendering myself and remaining open to what would come my way. I had to be the one to find the necessary resources here on earth that would help me. The universe will not wave a magic wand and make everything disappear as if nothing happened. The struggle is what makes us survive and grow wings...just like a butterfly struggling to escape the confines of its cocoon. If you were to help it along by breaking the shell for it to ease the struggle, the butterfly's wings would not have built up the necessary strength to be able to fly on its own and ultimately it would die. The struggle to get out is what gives the wings the necessary power to pull itself out of the dark confines of the cocoon into the free light of the day. The same goes with all life; we may not understand what exactly is going on through the hard times, but later we are able to recognize just how that hardship actually helped us along.

I had to learn to completely surrender to that Higher Power and let it take the wheel of my life and bring me to where it wanted me to be. I had to learn to trust in a power greater than myself. To accept truth is purely an individual matter. No one can spoon feed another. Each of us must choose the time, the place, and the amount of truth that we will accept. If an opportunity presents itself, you must be quick to seize it otherwise it will disappear and chances are it will not come your way again. This was a very hard lesson for me to learn because I kept looking to outer sources to help me when the reality was I had to save myself first. Then and only then, would the universe conspire to send things my way. In my case, it took me to stubbornly try to make it on my own until the day I could no longer move or take another step.

After leaving Whitehorse and working my way back to nursing at the Grey Nuns Hospital in Edmonton, it took about a year of trying to continue to live with an overloaded plate of trauma before it came crashing to a quick halt. One can only pretend that life is great for so long before the truth of the matter will come seeping through the very pores of your skin. I found myself looking to the sky again to come save me from myself. I decided to ask the Universe for a sign, an actual sign that it was time for me to change. I specifically said, "Alright! Enough of this guessing game! I need a sign...Something I can see with my very own eyes as proof that something needs to change in my life. I don't want intuition or a dream...I want a big, visual sign that I can actually see with my own eyes so I know that I am not making this up. Show me please." With that I hopped on the bus to go to work hoping I would get my sign.

30 minutes later, unbelievably as I looked out the window of the bus, there was a white billboard with the words written in big block letters, "IT'S TIME TO CHANGE!" It was a Nike advertisement. My jaw dropped with surprise and shock! I voiced out loud, "Is that my sign? That *IS* my sign! I can't believe this! WOW! That's my sign!" I kept craning my neck in order to get a better look at the billboard and kept rubbing my eyes to see if I was hallucinating. Nope! It was real and I knew it was for me! I was so excited and happy that my plea had been heard and I was given the actual sign I was looking for! I felt loved and for once had the actual physical proof that my Faith was accurate. I had to let that concept sink in for a while. What changes did it mean? I had to think about it.

Did this sign immediately change my behavior or my state of mind? Nope. Just because I now had the so called proof I needed, that doesn't mean I was ready to do something about it. I was quite content that now I had tangible evidence that someone out there in the Universe heard me. That was good enough for me, so I decided I would wait. Wait for what? I have no idea; I was just going to wait for the next sign I suppose. Well, that next sign came a week later when I made it to work the night shift and I looked at my patient list and simply could not read it! It was as if it was written in Chinese for all I knew. I rubbed my eyes and tried again, but it was all gibberish on my sheet; I knew right then and there, deep down in my heart that I was done. I had reached my limit of pretending everything was just fine in my life. There simply was no more room in my head to pretend that I was ok. It was time to change and do something for myself; the sign was right. But I just didn't know what or even how to start. I grabbed my jacket and immediately walked off the unit to make my way down to the Psychiatric Unit. On the way there, all my pain and sorrow came bubbling up like a geyser and I completely lost it sobbing uncontrollably. I got to the locked unit wanting them to commit me for insanity and started pounding on the door all the while screaming: "Let me in...Let me in!" They were calling security yelling, "Get her out! Get her out!" 2 security guards showed up and literally dragged me to Emergency Room to the "rubber room" under the watchful eye of a guard so I wouldn't hurt myself.

When the psychiatric Dr. finally showed up and assessed me, I told him my entire story and for the very first time in my life, I felt so relieved that I could finally get it out. It took 2 hours of me talking and him furiously taking notes. I was feeling quite satisfied and certain that he would tell me that I had multiple personality disorder, or that I was bi-polar, or possibly even schizophrenic...anything to commit me and give me some "happy pills". I was completely content with him diagnosing me as crazy and medicating me to be committed to a unit for further assessment. I had already accepted that as my fate and felt certain that they would most definitely find something terribly wrong with me, which would give me an excuse for my crazy and erratic behavior. As I prepared for him to tell me something of this nature, to my absolute shock, he tells me that it was his opinion that I have no mental health problems whatsoever! All I needed to do was to quit drinking and deal with the long list of problems that I had shared with him. I was stunned and replied, "What? Quit drinking? What in the world does my drinking alcohol have to do with anything? Did you not hear a word of what I just said about the years of sexual abuse and battery?" He said there were no magic pills that would take away the pain or trauma of what I had endured and alcohol only made it worse. Locking me up to a committed facility would serve absolutely no purpose. Until I quit drinking, nothing would change and any anti-depressant medication wouldn't work anyways. He said to quit the alcohol intake and go deal with the trauma. With that, he gave me information on AADAC and sent me home on the bus in bright yellow pajamas because they confiscated my hospital scrubs. Unbelievable! Now, not only did I feel like a psychiatric patient, I actually looked like one with my hair everywhere, my face swollen from crying and wearing my yellow pajamas on the bus....great! Just great!

I decided to take his advice and went to a 21-day treatment program with my work supporting me through this. The first homework that my counsellor gave me was a picture of an empty water bottle. She said the bottle represented me and asked me to write a traumatic event with the age it happened at every single line of the bottle starting from the bottom up. She gave me a week to do it and we would discuss it next time we met. For the very first time, I actually sat down and wrote every single thing that had ever happened to me. As I wrote, I could start to understand her point because the picture now had writings on both sides of the bottle and I actually had run out of space to write, so I had flipped the page over and continued writing. To see it on paper was certainly an eye opener! I represented the bottle and when I realized just how much the bottle was overflowing on both sides of the paper, it made me realize that maybe I truly needed some help after all. However, I was still quite surprised when the counsellor told me that 21 days wouldn't even touch the tip of the iceberg with me. She said I would need long-term treatment to address all my longstanding untreated trauma. The alcohol consumption was only masking what was underneath and where the real problems were. All the trauma that had been festering for so very long was boiling over and needed to be addressed soon. It was high time I dealt with it.

All the advice and signs in the world won't make one iota of a difference until the desire to change comes from deep within oneself. Clearly, I wasn't ready because I drank as soon as I got home and ultimately ended up getting fired from the hospital because of it. So, here I found myself with no income or possibility of getting hired anytime soon, my daughter wasn't speaking to me, I was running out of options for food and resources, and my brain couldn't seem to function any longer. Although I had the knowledge that I needed help, I couldn't seem to put two and two together. I just couldn't think clearly anymore and it's as if the blackness of depression surrounded my every waking moment. I was done. I had hit my rock bottom. I was at a crossroads in my life. What do I do and where do I go now? Where are you, God? Why don't you help me? Don't you hear my cries of pain and despair? Don't you read my heart full of despair and sorrow? It's as if I was expecting Him to wave a magic wand and poof! Everything would be OK. I laid on the couch and waited for God to save me.

I laid on that couch of my tiny basement suite for 3 days barely moving. I would stare for hours on end at the ceiling crying and crying. The darkness was swallowing me whole or so it seemed. I couldn't even be bothered to shower or comb my hair. I had lost all motivation to fight or even move. Surprisingly, when all faith seemed to have disappeared, and doubt was at its strongest, I had a Spiritual Experience of a Lifetime. When I was at my lowest, God showed up to guide my footsteps and show me the way once again. Why do I always continue to doubt?

I was on my knees praying and crying in the living room listening to the Foo Fighters "Skin & Bones" acoustic version DVD. A song came on called "Another Round" where the lyrics say: "We could just lay around, stare at the ceiling. Want to forget about, one for the feeling. Room full of photographs, box full of letters. Come on make it last, nothing else matters right now. Can you go another round? I will follow you down and out. Let's go another round I will follow you down and out." Well, I had just spent 3 days staring at the ceiling and looking through old photographs of my past, as well as reading old letters from years gone by. And now, nothing else seemed to matter to me but my misery. The song had hit the nail on the head so to say. So while I am on my knees crying my heart out, the chorus repeated, "Can you go another round? I will follow you down and out...." The words were repeated again and again. Throughout my despair, the words finally sunk in and I actually stopped to listen to question myself if I could go another round? "Can I? Do I have the strength?" I was contemplating this very question when I looked up at the very tiny kitchen window, which was completely covered with stuff outside so absolutely no light could get through. To my complete surprise, a ray of light came through the darkness. It was the size of a Canadian two dollar coin, and was filled with pinpointed stars of all colors of pinks, purple, yellow, blue, orange and white. The stars would slowly spin around and around as they moved towards my heart center. The seemingly magical ray of light touched me and I felt a tingle all over. I looked up at the window where this ray was coming from, then down to my heart area where the beam had made its home. At the same time, I could hear the words to the song playing, "Can you go another round? I will follow you." Still mistrusting and having to prove once again the existence of God, I said, "Really? We will see about that..." I got up and moved to the kitchen; lo and behold if the light, seemingly glued to my heart center, followed me! Unbelievable! So I moved to the couch, stood on it and jumped up and down. The light followed all of my movements! I couldn't believe my eyes! How can this be? Everywhere I went in that tiny apartment, the light followed my every movement! The words of the song kept playing over and over while I moved around. Finally, it sunk in that I wasn't alone. If I could find the strength to continue my fight for survival, I would have the help I would need. I instantly fell back to my knees in surrender and said aloud, "OK. I will try again." As I cried in complete and utter surrender, and wondering what my next step would be, in that instant, I heard a voice say," Kathy! Get up! Get up!" I looked around to see who had spoken, but I was alone. Without further questioning anything, I stood up and immediately heard a knock on the door. It was my friend Don who lived upstairs coming to see if I was ok. He said he had an inner nudge to come check on me. I told him I wasn't ok, so he brought me to a place where I could get the help I so desperately needed. I am grateful that he actually listened to that inner voice telling him to come and check on me. Thank you, Don!

It was in that moment of vulnerability and surrender that I was able to open myself up to a Higher Power and receive the gifts coming my way. I ended up going to a year-long Christian women's recovery program given through the Hope Mission called Wellsprings. It was by far the very best thing I could have ever done for myself. It was there that I learned for the very first time about Boundaries and Codependency. Pretty sad that I had to learn about it at the age of 40, but at least I finally understood the pattern of behavior that had consistently followed me throughout my life. I understood the why behind my decisions and choices. I learned that I actually had a choice; I never knew I did prior to this program. I had simply gone along with whatever circumstance came my way; I felt as if I had lived under a rock most of my life. Where had I been all these years?

I would love to say that I never had another drink again, but I had some more "research" to do before I was completely done with alcohol. I relapsed a few weeks after leaving the program and this led me to another level of darkness that I hadn't experienced yet. This relapse lasted for a year of me pretending everything was ok and that I could handle my drinking because I had just spent 9 months in treatment and had dealt with my issues of sexual abuse. NOT! This time I ended up in the hospital with my arm slashed in a drunken episode that I have no recollection. All I know is that my daughter left and returned to the safety of her father's again; I lost my nursing job once again, and this time I was evicted. Now I had no job, an angry daughter, no money and no home! Who would have ever guessed that "Rock Bottom" had a basement? I put whatever things I had left into a storage unit and was homeless for a week until once again something changed.

That week of being completely homeless and walking the streets was life changing for me. My brain was literally in a fog with shock and denial. I stumbled around not knowing what to do or how to go about this new level of rock bottom. I was in a place surrounded by 100+ other lost souls, and could only lay half on the table at the Drop-In center with my head in my arms. There was no more tears; only darkness and hopelessness. I would lift my head and look around me to see the ugliness of where I found myself and ask, "How in the world did I end up here?" I am educated and smart; so why am I here surrounded by all these sad Souls? How did I let it get this far? On the seventh day, I was following around "Toothless Joe", a man well known on the streets for his savviness of where to find things for survival. As we walked along, he very happily slapped me hard on the back and said, "This is the life! Live it! Enjoy it!" The fog that was clouding my every thought suddenly dissipated and a clarity of mind appeared out of nowhere. It was a clarity

I had not experienced in a long while, and it was as if that hard slap on my back had completely shaken up my thoughts and rearranged them. Incredulously, I was stunned by what he said and looked at him as if he were an alien. I said, "What did you say?" so he repeated it with a great big toothless smile and laugh. Time stopped as his words sunk in and I finally recognized my situation. Thank God that cloud of darkness had suddenly lifted long enough for me to see clearly. With a conviction that came from the very depths of my Soul, I replied, "THIS IS NOT MY LIFE!" I actually stomped my foot and said it even louder, "THIS IS SO NOT MY LIFE!" With that statement, I made a decision right then and there that this was NOT how my story was going to end. If he was accepting of the circumstances, well I most certainly wasn't! Heck no! I didn't care what I had to do to fix things, but spending the rest of my days in the company of 'Toothless Joe' just wasn't an option for me. I drew the line on this part. I had absolutely no idea of where I was going or how I was going to get there; all I knew is what I *didn't* want....and that was being in the current situation I found myself in. With that official decision, I turned around and walked straight to the hospital where I remained for a few weeks detoxing from alcohol, until I was discharged and went straight back to Wellsprings Recovery Program. Clearly, I had missed a few things, and I was bound and determined to go figure it out. Hanging around with Toothless Joe was not an option for me and I would do whatever it took to not ever return to that nightmare!

I remained in the recovery program for women another 5 months where I was finally able to address all the guilt and shame I had in reserve with my daughter. The first time round, I had dealt with all the sexual abuse and violence I endured, but there were many more layers to uncover; just like an onion with layers and layers to peel away at. I had been so broken by life that I had no idea what I even liked or disliked so this time was very precious to me. It was a place of healing and discovery and left feeling confident that I would be ok. It was in recovery that I met the man of my dreams and thought that love was the answer. I quickly learned that love alone will NOT keep you sober! True recovery comes from a place deep within yourself and not from the arms of another person. Everything sacred in life has to come from deep within; you have to somehow learn to tap into that inner source of strength and let it fill your being in order to guide your steps in life. I do it through daily contemplation and singing HU for 20 minutes a day. Learn to go inside yourself, because this is the Source of all Truth. There are a lot of holy temples out there, but the most sacred of all is the temple inside you because this is where you meet with the Holy Spirit, the Voice of God. How do you meet with the Holy Spirit? If you come from Christianity, you pray. You come to the Holy temple, to the holy of holies, through prayer. You meet on holy ground with your God. If you are a member of any other religion, you have a means of going to that holy of holies, whether it's meditation or contemplation or prayer. Go to the holy of holies. It's the temple inside you. This is the place where all truth comes from. Before there were words, before there was a written Bible or a printed Gutenberg Bible, before there was Luther's translation, there was the Word in the heart of mankind. This is the temple. Go there.[13] As Jesus said, "The Kingdom of Heaven lies within." Find what works for you. Not everything the same will work for each and every person out there. Do whatever works and makes you feel good. For me, it's singing the HU, an ancient name for God. However, let it be said here that prayer alone gave me strength, but did not keep me sober; love did not keep me sober; promises to my daughter that I would change could

---

13   Beyond Meditation – Spiritual Experiences Guidebook

not keep me sober. I still had to figure out why I kept relapsing when I thought I had done everything right by sharing all my traumatic stories. When I left Wellsprings for the 2nd time, I moved in with Roland and lived a fairy-tale existence believing that love would keep me sober and everything would be amazingly great. NOT!

After losing another and ultimately my last nursing job, I sank into another depression and struggled with my alcohol intake once again. This was the second time I relapsed after treatment and I had run out of avenues of hope. Even though my fiancé was extremely loving and supporting, I was the one with the problem. I didn't understand where this continuous cycle kept coming from. I thought that love was the cure; I had dealt with my trauma and my guilt so what was left? Seriously? How many flipping layers did I have? It was after a 6-month relapse of extreme daily drinking that I had a dream that changed my perception on life.

I dreamt that I was visiting another era in the time of Atlantis, where a group of women wearing long white dresses approached me in an extremely welcoming manner. Their skin was a silky brown color and their luxurious, chestnut hair and flowed to their knees. Their beauty was golden and they exuded a light that doesn't exist in this world. They welcomed me singing in hymns and as if I were royalty. I was having a difficult time understanding their words so a giant, old yellowed scroll suddenly appeared and hung in mid-air so I could read the words they were saying. It read:

"Kathy, you must not drink alcohol anymore! God needs you in one year's time and you simply cannot drink any longer! For with every ounce of alcohol that touches your lips, 1000 people are affected nega-tively by it." In that moment, I was lifted above and saw myself with a ripple effect of negativity exuding from me in a wide circle. The ripples were black in color and what I was putting out there was extremely dark and negative. It went on to read, "However, with every ounce of love that you sow, you will affect 100,000 people in a positive way." I was drawn up above once again, and this time I saw myself surrounded by ripples of the colors of pink, orange, yellow and white. These ripples extended as far as I could see all around me in a positive way and touched every Soul near me. The scroll went on to say that in one year's time, I had a special mission to accomplish and that I must NOT be drinking ANY alcohol. The ladies told me that they have been following me for thousands of years and only allowed me to remember this dream because of the importance of it. They said they would continue to monitor my progress and with that, I awoke in a state of complete wonder. I haven't had a drink of alcohol since this dream due to the visual impact of seeing the ripple effect of my actions on others. I finally realized just how powerful our actions, thoughts, and deeds affect all those around us either in a positive or negative way. This powerful dream changed my beliefs about what I do with myself and how I can affect others, even without realizing it. I had no idea of the great impact our actions can have on those closest to us. This was enough for me and thankfully, I have been sober since. Not to mention who was I to disobey God? If I am told that I am needed for a mission for God then I will most certainly not be the one who will disobey and thus be turned into stone just like in the Bible. No way! This dream was so real and so very powerful that I felt to disobey would forever condemn me to hell on earth. I received God's message loud and clear and finally, finally understood the depths of my actions and the effect on others. (I do have to mention here that *exactly* one year to the date of this dream, I got the call to be hired in the Northern Alberta Oil Sands - thus changing my life forever!)

I did return to recovery one last time in order to figure out why I kept relapsing regardless of all the hard work I had put in to-date. I used the center this time as my own personal Tibetan Monastery and focused all my energy in to figuring out who I really was. I found out during a deep EMDR (Eye Movement Desensitization and Reprocessing) LED Light Treatment session. These sessions have the person follow a red LED light back and forth with therapist leading you down memory lane. It has a record of assisting clients with addiction issues at a success rate of 75%. It was worth a try for me. The therapist asked me to remember as far back as I possibly could to where this feeling of worthlessness comes from. I replied from the age of 4 because of the sexual abuse. Then she asked me if I have ever felt worthy? I was about to say no, when all of a sudden the very first dream I had with Jesus when I was 12 came rushing back in my memory. It was in that loving memory that I recognized that Jesus thought I was worthy because I was one of the few that could actually go to him, while most people were frozen to the spot! A lightbulb went off in my head! Ding! Ding! Ding! In the very next second, every single God moment I have ever had in the course of my lifespan to date, (and there have been thousands of these moments) came flooding into my awareness and the sheer magnitude of it left an impact that shook me to the core and still remains to this date! It was in that moment of clarity that I recognized that I exist because God loves me and thus I said: "Who cares what man thinks of me? Is the opinion of a human being more important to me than the opinion of the Almighty God? As long as God thinks I am worthy, I will be ok!" From that moment on, I have been fine and my personal journey of recovery has remained solid since. Other people's opinions of me have no effect whatsoever on me now. If someone doesn't like me...oh well and so what? I am not here to please people on earth, and I will no longer base my decisions and live my life according to someone else's ideas or opinions. I am finally free of that trap thankfully! Today I do the best I can and be the best I can, and I strive to better myself every single day. I do it for me and not to please someone else. Talk about freedom! If you can learn to step out of your own way on your path to success, it will open up doors that you never knew existed. We truly can be our own biggest obstacles just by the negative self-beliefs that we carry around with us everywhere we go. Tell yourself today that you will no longer stop yourself from trying new and scary things. Tell yourself that today you will push yourself to make that phone call you have bee procrastinating about for so long. Tell yourself today that you will do the best you can, be the best you can and love yourself the best you can. What doesn't get done today, you can always pick up tomorrow. Remember to be kind to your mind as you are in control of your thoughts – make them good ones!

"When God calls you to do something, He enables you to do it."

~Robert Schuller~

STOP & REFLECT:

1. Has there ever been a time in your life where something out of the ordinary happened to you that you can't explain? And even if you did, you felt the experience was so extraordinary that no-one would believe you?

_____

_____

_____

_____

_____

_____

2. Faith is a very personal matter and a journey of self-discovery. What I believe in isn't necessarily what you believe in. Have you discovered what it is you believe in and what holds you together through the hard times?

_____

_____

_____

_____

_____

_____

3. Here is a small list of things some spiritual experiences. Check the ones you have already experienced in the past.

- Prophetic dream/dreams that were so real you thought they happened
- Déjà vu/past-life memory
- Flying in your dreams/ dreaming of far-off yet wonderful places
- Out-of-body or near-death experience
- Dreams with a departed loved one
- Inner light(s)/Inner sound
- Intuition: direct knowingness
- Sense of oneness or loving presence
- Miracles: healing, protection, guidance
- Guidance from angels. Spiritual guides, departed loved ones

4. What Spiritual Experience have you had that has changed your perception of how life works here in the physical sense?

_____

_____

_____

_____

_____

_____

5. How do connect your Spiritual Experiences that come in your dreams with your everyday life? Do you understand the co-relation of just how the two really are connected? Write in the space below how the dots connect between the two worlds.

_____

_____

_____

_____

_____

_____

_____

_____

_____

_____

_____

_____

_____

_____

_____

_____

_____

Chapter 9:

WINDS OF CHANGE

GOAL SETTING:

The definition of goal setting is the process of identifying something that you want to accomplish and establishing measurable goals and timeframes. Goal setting is a powerful process for thinking about your ideal future, and for motivating yourself to turn your vision of this future into reality. It helps you choose where you want to go in life.

Goal setting involves the development of an action plan designed to motivate and guide a person or group toward a goal. Goal setting can be guided by goal-setting criteria (or rules) such as SMART criteria: Specific, Measurable, Attainable, Relevant, and Time-Bound. Goal setting is a major component of personal development.[14]

I don't think I had ever written down a goal in my entire life until now. I would set them in my mind and work towards them like when I decided to be a model and move to Montreal, Miami or New York. My goal to move to Jasper or to become a nurse despite what people would say about it was never written down; it was simply a decision that I acted upon. My precious time in Wellsprings gave me the

---

14   From Wikipedia, the free encyclopedia

necessary time away from the stresses of the world to actually think about what I wanted in life. I wrote down who and what I wanted to be when I grew up, and the steps necessary to get there. Doing this was a very important step in my recovery. I had to start from scratch and actually take my goals and turn them into achievements. I couldn't do this without having to learn first about how to not only *survive*, but how *to live*; I had to learn about boundaries, codependency, anger management, and especially self-care. When I was approached with the topic of anger management, I laughed and said I didn't need that because I never had an angry episode in my life and I steered clear of anyone angry. The counsellor looked at me and told me I especially needed the class because of my lack of acknowledgment towards the subject. Anger comes out in many sneaky and different ways such as depression, isolation, self-loathing, as well as eating disorders. Angry thoughts react physically and may be accompanied by muscle tension, headaches or an increased heart rate. I was the kind of person who never knew I was angry until I went to that class. Boy what a surprise that was when I finally figured out that I was one angry lady who had internally let it fester an entire lifetime! I had to write many letters of aggression towards all those who had hurt me and it wasn't pretty. I cried some hard tears releasing all that nastiness inside me and made many a trip to the gym to release some of that pent up anger. Boy! What a relief to discover something so crucial, and being able to live the feelings instead of repressing it or replacing it with something different. I was free at last to recognize what I was feeling, experience it, and then let it go. WOW!

It took time to discover exactly who Kathy was, and what I wanted to be when I grew up at the age of 42. The hardest part was letting go of the identity I had created for myself as a nurse. I had put everything I was and what I believed what was right for me into my nursing career. Take that away, and now what do I do? Who am I really without that title attached to my name? I had no idea...I truly didn't. I felt naked and raw, bleeding from the inside out and completely stripped of identity and purpose. The everlasting age-old questions of "Who am I? What am I doing here?" came creeping up on me when I least expected it. How does one change careers at midlife and completely start over? Where do I start and where do I go from here? So many questions and no answers that would come quick enough for me. Letting go of the identity I had created for myself through nursing felt like shedding a layer of skin, stepping out of the old and into something new. My problem was that I just didn't have something new to step into yet, thus the feeling of being vulnerable, raw and utterly exposed.

Still in recovery, I ended up going to a free 3-day career workshop that offered aptitude and personality tests to match you up with a possible career choice. By the end of it, the facilitator gave me my personal match and I just about fell off my chair! I looked up at her and told her she gave me the wrong one; that this couldn't possibly be mine. It said that my match was that of a Heavy Equipment Operator! Impossible! That was a man's job and I was a woman who was 42 at the time. I had never even looked at equipment or paid attention because that was so not who I was. How could this be even possible? I was geared to caregiving careers along the lines of nursing, or so I thought. The aptitude test was wrong and I told her that. She calmly looked at me and said it was right; I only needed to believe in myself a little and I would see. She immediately put on a video of Les Brown on "It's Possible" and the seed was planted that maybe, just maybe I could do it. Just because I had never done it before doesn't mean that I didn't have the ability to learn. I knew I was a good driver, so I slowly started to believe that maybe she was right. I was empowered by Les Brown's video, so I decided I had nothing to lose so may as well give it a try. I was on the bottom so the only way I could go was up. Les Brown says, "If you fall and land on your back looking up, then you can get up!" I figured I would give it a try and I took that scary first step into something new and terrifying for me.

The facilitator sent me to Women Building Futures whose main objective is to get women into the trades. I looked them up online and decided that maybe this would be a good change for me. I was going to go to the next available information session on the following Wednesday, but my gut feeling and intuition were screaming at me to go on Friday instead. The feeling was so strong and powerful that I had no choice but to listen. I learned a very long time ago to follow my gut instincts as they were *always* right. I am so very glad that I did. I went there early on Friday morning for their information session, and the lady said while I was waiting I could look over what they had just received that very morning, an offer of a pilot project from Imperial Oil. It was a 12-week program for Heavy Equipment Operator for 16 women to *possibly* be hired for a Heavy Haul Truck Operator. It would be a camp job on a 10 day on, 10 days off rotation. I just happened to be the very first woman to be offered a chance at this amazing opportunity as it was hot off the press...literally, the paper was hot to touch from just being printed. I took one look at the offer and immediately said," Oh My! I'll take that!" I was originally going to take the offer from Lafarge to become a Class 1 cement truck driver, but this new offer was way better and I knew it was the right choice for me. Had I went to Women Building Futures on Wednesday like I was going to, I would've completely missed the opportunity offered by Imperial Oil. I am so very thankful that I learned to listen to my intuition years ago and that I followed it.

I sat through the information session and a seed was firmly planted that this was going to be my new path. I would do whatever it took to get this offer and would apply myself tenaciously until I was accepted. Although I had many, many obstacles to overcome, I put my mind to it and set myself up for success. I even put up a picture in my closet of a Heavy Haul Truck that I had found, so that I could look at my goal every single day to inspire me to work harder for it. I had to pass a math test, and I knew math was always a "not so good" subject for me, never mind the fact I hadn't done math in 20 years. The ladies at WBF said all I needed was 50% to pass, but really, are they going to pick someone who has low 50's% or someone who has high 80's%? To me it was obvious; get a good grade! I took math tutoring through P.A.L.S., a free service to assist those struggling in Math and English. During the day I worked on my recovery, and every single night, I would pour over algebra, equations, percentages, fractions, and problem solving. It was painful and difficult for me and I would have a headache every single day because of it, but I persisted. I ended up getting a 96% in math because of all my hard work, and was so happy that I did a complete body floor slide across the kitchen floor of my small apartment in Wellsprings home. My roommate, Taanis Ryan, was bent over laughing at me and wondered if I lost my mind as she looked at me on the floor not understanding the magnitude of what just occurred.

Every little step I took for myself seemed to me a giant step in the grand scope of things. My self-esteem was so very shaky that it seemed to take an enormous amount of effort to do what I needed to do for myself. From an outsider's perspective looking in, my accomplishments may have seemed trivial, but to me, it was a major mountain that I had just climbed! The winds of change were blowing through me and slowly changing my own views about myself. I was beginning to believe in myself again and disregard all the lies that I had been told my entire life. I was beginning to blossom, shine and grow into an incredibly beautiful and strong woman. I still remained reluctant to believe it, but as the various tests for WBF continued and I passed them all, the belief that maybe, just maybe I could do this began to plant its roots deep into my subconscious.

I was having recurring dreams that I was training up in a mine driving Haul Trucks even before I was accepted into the program. I had a dream 2 months before I was accepted into the program about a big "Congratulations! You have been accepted!" These constant dreams gave me the confidence I needed to put even more effort into going above and beyond what the expectations were. I received notification on Dec 21st that I had been accepted into the upcoming program that was to start in February. There were 170 women that had applied and I was one of the 16 chosen! Unbelievable! Wow! I cried and I cried of sheer joy and happiness for once. I did it! I had a chance at a new beginning and I wasn't going to blow it this time.

The program started and it was overwhelming, to say the least. I looked at the other women and my low self-esteem immediately told me that I was inadequate and beneath them. This low self-esteem was pushing me to believe the old lies that had haunted me for my entire life. I had to constantly talk myself into believing that I was worthy of this and was a good driver so I did belong in this opportunity. That negative and limiting self-belief was like a shadow constantly overlooking my shoulder. It was ever-present and would show up when I least expected it coming to haunt my every move. What a battle it was to overpower it by self-talking my way through it. Exhausting, actually. The constant battle of the mind was ever present in my life. I am my own biggest obstacle in my life, therefore, it is up to me to fight my way through my own negative thoughts. The Ultimate Championship Fight of a lifetime!

Those 12 weeks were by far the best thing that could have ever happened to me because it slowly gave me confidence that I could accomplish something this big. Every little step I took was a building block to step on and feel better about myself. I fearfully got on the bulldozer but I operated it as if I had previously been on one. How can this be? I couldn't believe just how much I loved everything about this program. It gave me a self-confidence I never knew I had. Driving the rock truck was a blast with my new friend Diana cheering me on with loads of positive reinforcement; that simple action helped me tremendously! Thank you, Diana, you beautiful Soul, for encouraging me when I needed it the most. When it came to the grader, my friend and now co-worker Tiina Onnis went ahead of me and was yelled at for an hour by the instructor about wrecking the $8000 transmission. He was an old army guy and to hear him yell at her over the radio sent a wave of fear through me. I knew I wasn't ready to handle being yelled at, especially in front of so many other people. I was terrified because it was my turn the next morning. Tiina was a true champion and to her, this event was nothing. As she stepped off the grader, she smiled at the instructor and said, "That wasn't so bad...I did pretty good! So...what's the next piece of equipment I can get on?" His face turned purple and he actually hopped up and down in exasperation and frustration reminding me of Samite Sam in the Bugs Bunny cartoons, while Tiina just grinned her mischievous smile truly enjoying his display of emotions. "I think I did pretty well," she said with a smile; while knowing full well that she almost gave the man a heart attack! If only he could see her now and how well she operates the 24 M Grader; she works it like the pro she is! Way to go Tiina!

I went home in a panic that day because I was next in line and really couldn't handle being yelled at, so I went on YouTube and studied every single grader training video since 1972! I sat there for 4 hours watching, observing and studying everything there was to know about the grader. By the time I actually got on the piece of equipment, I operated that thing like I had been doing it for some time! That same instructor who had yelled at Tiina, was beaming and smiling so much his cheeks were red. He was glowing with pride so much that he made it a point of telling WBF how good I was who in turn, told Imperial Oil. My only concern at the time was that he didn't yell at me; operating it well came second. I was just so relieved he didn't yell at me that I didn't care about anything else.

The first time I operated an excavator and was loading a rock truck, the instructor was jumping up and down happily yelling how well I was doing and that he couldn't believe I had never operated an excavator before! The three other women who were waiting their turn were screaming with glee and cheering me on in encouragement. It was in that moment, I understood that I was free of the lies that plagued me throughout my life. It didn't matter to me if I was ultimately chosen or not for the opportunity presented because my self-confidence was building and I suddenly believed and trusted that I would be ok. I knew that I wasn't "a waste of skin" or "a useless piece of crap" and I now knew that I absolutely did not "pollute the very air around me" Who says that anyways? Worse yet is that I believed those lies! Not anymore. In that instant, I was freed from those negative and haunting beliefs about myself. That day as I walked home, a song played on my iPod called "Redeemed" by Big Daddy Weave and I immediately felt released from everything I had been carrying around for so very long. The lyrics to the song were exactly what I had been experiencing for my entire life about carrying past shame, guilt and feelings of unworthiness and now how I had just been "Redeemed". A weight had suddenly been lifted from my shoulders and I no longer had doubts about my future. I *believed in myself* for the first time in years and boy what a feeling! For every piece of equipment I operated, it was as if I had done it previously and all 3 instructors commented on it. To see them believe in me helped me a long way on my journey of recovery. When I say recovery, I don't mean with alcohol. Alcohol was only a disguise for the underlying cause of pain and despair. Recovery in the sense of who I was as a person discovering myself for the first time of my life. Recovery from the broken pieces of a shattered life and personal image. Every step I took, every little thing that I did for myself, was a stepping stone to rebuild the foundation from scratch; another piece of the puzzle of Kathy being put back together. Thus, the 12-week Heavy Equipment Operator course played a huge role in this rebuilding phase. Every little accomplishment while operating was a huge success on my part and yet another piece of the puzzle was added towards the end result. To see all the other women succeed in learning to operate and obtain that self-confidence was a beautiful thing to watch. I am very thankful for the opportunity given to me.

Out of the 16 of us, only 11 were chosen to go work up in the Northern Alberta Oil Sands. The stress was high and time ticked away ever so slowly as we waited to hear back from the interviews. My interview had gone well I thought even though I only had nursing situations to refer to. One of the interviewers, Gerry, told me he heard I was really good on the grader from WBF as well as the instructor, so he asked me about it. I told him exactly what I did with watching all the training videos prior and it impressed the heck out them both apparently. They saw it as an initiative for learning, while I saw it as self-preservation in getting out of a situation where I would get yelled at. Too funny!

A week later, my fiancé and I were so broke that we were actually heading out to go cash in on our empty bottles when I received a call from an unknown number. I decided I had better take the call and boy am I glad I did! It was Gerry, the man who interviewed me. He said he was calling because he would like to give me a verbal offer of employment and asked if I wanted to accept it? I screamed so loud in excitement that I am sure the neighbor's down the street heard me! I stopped and began to cry loudly I was so overjoyed with delight. I suddenly stopped crying and asked," Is this a crank call? Who is this and how did you get my number? If this is a joke it isn't funny!" He laughed heartily and told me to sit down because he was going to tell me just how much money I would be making and didn't want me to pass out and hurt myself! I spoke with him for a good 20 minutes then looked over at Roland and told him to put down the bottles because we were going to be ok. We went for a drive for a few hours to absorb this new information and how it would change our lives and all the positive things that would come out of it. I thanked God over and over again still afraid to believe that this was really happening to me. I was ever so grateful that it did and refused to ponder it further. I accepted my new date with destiny with wide open arms. Look out world, here I come!

Setting goals for ourselves is an absolute must. It gives our lives direction and purpose. It will drive you to push yourself to succeed beyond your wildest expectations. Start with small goals and when you achieve them you are empowered to try bigger and more difficult ones. For me, the challenge was to persist regardless of the obstacles put on my path and believe me, there have been too many to mention here. The positive feeling of overcoming a challenging situation you thought was overwhelming, will leave you feeling as if you just climbed Mount Everest! You will be empowered to try something a little harder next time because now you have some self-confidence to help you along. Confidence will give you what the phone booth gave Clark Kent in Superman! It will give you wings to fly on and soar the winds of change like you created it! Make this your mission in life; to allow yourself to feel good about YOU! The key to goal setting success is to imagine it being accomplished already; feel it and experience it as if it were already materialized; visualize it and hold the image in your mind until it happens. Put a picture of what you want on your desk, wall or mirror so you can see it every day and strive to work towards it a little bit every day. Trust your intuition and prepare for what you ask for and be very specific and careful what you ask for because remember that you just might get it!

I think it noteworthy to talk a bit about making excuses. I made excuses most of my life and blamed many others instead of looking at myself for a change in attitude and behaviour. Excuses are another form of roadblocks we commonly use. Excuses make it easier to justify and give up on a dream so we feel better about not fighting for what we believe in. By making excuses we give up responsibility for our goal and the problem it never solved. My question to you is how valid is your excuse? Take a minute a re-evaluate what it is exactly that you tell yourself each and every day as to why you are not working towards your goals and dreams? Here are some common excuses that I know I have personally used in the past:

- I'm not smart enough
- I'm not good enough
- I'm not pretty enough
- I'm too fat and too shy
- I don't have time
- I'm too tired
- No one believes in me
- I don't believe in me
- I'm too old
- I don't have the money

What are the damaging words you use against yourself to prevent you from achieving that ever so important goal in life? There is ALWAYS a solution. Tell yourself that you are always only one idea away from solving whatever obstacle is in your path. Remember to watch what you tell yourself because YOU are listening!

"We must look to be an active force in our own lives. We must take charge of our own destinies; design a life of substance and truly begin to live our dreams."

~Les Brown~

STOP & REFLECT:

1. An important benefit of setting goals isn't always achieving it, it's what you do with the person *you become* in order to achieve your goal that is the real benefit. What is your current goal? What is your timeline to achieve it?

_____

_____

_____

_____

_____

_____

2. Goal setting is powerful because it provides focus and it will shape your dreams. What are the next three steps you need to take to attain your goal?

_____

_____

_____

_____

_____

_____

3. Identifying potential obstacles can help you plan ways to deal with them. Before you can remove a roadblock, you have to recognize the problem. Once you are able to take responsibility for the roadblock, you will be able to think of ways to get around it. What are your potential obstacles?

_____

_____

_____

_____

_____

4. Now that you have recognised the potential roadblocks, what is your plan to overcome them? What steps do you need to take to tackle and conquer them? List them below.

_____

_____

_____

_____

5. Find a picture of your goal, or even draw one and put it somewhere you can see it every day. Stick in on the fridge if you have to, as long as you see it as a reminder on the hard days what you are trying to accomplish. Give yourself a visual reminder to push yourself when you don't feel like it.

Chapter 10:

LIVING TRUTH

WISDOM:

Wisdom is the ability to think and act using knowledge, experience, understanding, common sense, and insight. The quality or state of being wise; knowledge of what is true or right coupled with just judgment as to action; sagacity, discernment, or insight.

Wisdom has been regarded as one of four cardinal virtues; and as a virtue, it is a habit or disposition to perform the action with the highest degree of adequacy under any given circumstance with the limitation of error in any given action. This implies a possession of knowledge, or the seeking of knowledge to apply to the given circumstance. This involves an understanding of people, objects, events, situations, and the willingness as well as the ability to apply perception, judgment, and action in keeping with the understanding of what is the optimal course of action. In short, wisdom is a disposition to find the truth coupled with an optimum judgment as to what actions should be taken.[15]

---

15   From Wikipedia, the free encyclopedia

Living my own truth has been the ultimate success in my life story. Having the ability to live honestly and truthfully without the disguise of many different masks to cover the layers of darkness beneath. Going from a place of slavery to one of personal mastery has been the challenge of a lifetime and the greatest personal achievement I could ever hope to aspire. Learning to stand on my own two feet has been a journey that is never-ending as I continue to fight my way through the constant trials and tribulations that life throws at me. The difference now is that I don't cower and hide beneath the false pretense alcohol provides, nor do I remain in the shadow of others. I am able to stand and face head on whatever comes my way and weather the storm without the fear of sinking in deep, dark waters. Not only do I remain afloat, but I can swim against the powerful waves and still keep my head above water. Is it easy? No. Do I still have fear and insecurities? Absolutely. The difference today is what I do with the obstacles or even the opportunities that come my way. It is my personal mindset which I believe sets me apart from many. It is my drive to pull myself out of the depths of darkness into the shining light of success that makes me who I am today. It is my motto that in life if you feel you don't succeed, then redefine success! Success will be what you make it and how you perceive it. My personal success is having the sheer will of not only survival but one of learning to live a prosperous life again despite all odds. Be fearless in the pursuit of what sets your Soul on fire! Find your passion; your drive; that one thing that makes you get dressed to face the day. The fire that's inside of me burns brighter than any fire than any outside force and this, I believe, is my driving strength. I joke with my co-workers that if they see a glow from the other end of the mine at night, not to worry because it's just my light shining and showing the way!

Learning to work in an environment that is mostly men was very difficult for me due to the trauma men have caused me in the past. I could've easily been intimidated and there are times when I most definitely was. But I refused to let that stop my growth. I am stronger than any fear I may have, so ultimately I am the one with the power to overcome it. I have learned that most men are good and kind, it's the level of tolerance that is accepted that makes the difference when it comes to abuse. The choice is mine on how I deal with things; either I let fear rule me or I use my KA-POW! (Kathy Power) and crush it with my double Hulk fists. I have spent my entire life living in fear and I simply refuse to do it any longer. Today I am able to be the kind of woman that when my feet hit the floor in the morning, the Devil says: "OH NO! SHE'S UP! It's going to be a busy day!"

My last story of personal success was when I was still in the first few months of driving that giant beast of a truck and my self-esteem was very shaky still. I had to bring the truck through the gates of a main traffic road to the maintenance yard, and the traffic lights were still not working. I had to call the security guards to block the entrance of the road so no light vehicles could go through while I drove through the intersection. As I am driving along, I noticed there was a long line up of vehicles coming from both directions that had been stopped by security. It was a hot sunny day and for some reason, a few people were getting out of their vehicles while they waited, maybe to smoke a cigarette. Time seemed to slow down considerably as I inched my way towards the gates. I observed the scene from both directions and watched people admire the sheer size of the truck I was driving. I could see the admiration of the faces of the onlookers as they were probably wishing to be in my place right at the moment. Suddenly, out of nowhere a wave of memories flooded my vision. All I could see was some of the most violent and humiliating scenes of my life, and I could hear all the nasty words that went with it on how useless I was and that I would never amount to anything. I could hear the replay of ugliness as I was referred to as a useless waste of skin; a worthless piece of crap and the many other nasty words used to describe me. They seemed to loom all around me attempting to swallow me whole. I could almost visualize the very words in letters surrounding me as I slowly made my way through the intersection. In that very crucial moment in time given to me with a new clarity of mind I had never before experienced, I simply refused to let the pages of my past come haunt my story of all my tomorrows. I smashed every single one of those thoughts out the window to the onlookers below. Instead, I reveled in just how much I had fought to be driving this giant truck across this road with all these people staring in awe. The people were looking at the truck and had nothing to do with who was operating it, but for me, in that moment, I was free! I mean completely free from all the slavery I had endured and in recognition of it, I looked down at the people who seemed to be lined up for a parade, and I totally did "The Queen Wave!" I looked around, smiled and waved just like I was the Queen of England! Never mind being a Princess, I sat tall and waved like I was the Queen! I looked both directions and smiled like I had never smiled before with tears of sheer joy streaming down my face. The moment was purifying for me; it was a cleansing that allowed me to be completely rid of all old negative self-limiting beliefs. Yet another layer was shed with a new beginning in the life of Kathy and the way she held herself. Amazing transformation in the works and am so grateful for every living experience I am given. I no longer am a prisoner of my past, plain and simple.

It seems like my life is full of new beginnings, and really it is because I choose to make every day count now. For the reader, think of every moment as an opportunity for you to tell yourself that this is *NOT* how your story is going to end. Every single minute that goes by is another opportunity to make a change within yourself. Time trickles away and most people don't even realize it until it is too late. They sit on the couch watching useless TV programs or playing X-Box/ PlayStation games as the clock is ticking away ever so slowly. The problem is that you think you have time. Don't spend your life wasting precious time on the hopes that you will have the time or the freedom to do it later. My years in nursing have taught me that time is a precious commodity which we take for granted. Don't waste it; make every second count. My hope for you is that you take the necessary time needed to make whatever changes you need to lead a better and happier life. Don't do it for your spouse; your kids; your parents; your teachers...do it for the most important person on the planet. YOU! YOU ARE IMPORTANT! Don't ever forget that.

If you are hurting in your life right now for whatever reason, I believe the key is to forgive what has happened in your life as well as those who may have hurt you. You will never forget it, but you can learn to live with yourself. Today is a different day and you can choose how that day will turn out. Only <u>YOU</u> can figure out what <u>YOU</u> need. I threw myself into changing my life and didn't worry about anyone else but Kathy. I tackled every obstacle that came my way...and believe me, obstacles WILL come! But I never gave up; I never let go of that light at the end of the tunnel that we so desperately try to reach. Set yourselves goals that are attainable; the feeling you get when you reach them is incredible! There are no words to describe crying tears of joy for once! Today I am truly happy with my life and everything in it. The miracles that happen in my life continue to amaze me and they still keep on coming. I have learned to love again and to be able to ACCEPT IT which is a very important step when fighting low self-esteem. Today I no longer survive; I LIVE! I had to learn to raise my standards, change my limiting beliefs and develop life skills all over again. I had to stop and ask myself," What can I do for myself today?" I still ask myself that question every single day.

You most certainly have had challenges in the past as we all do, but I am asking you to recognize that if you continue to push yourself to change your situation, at some point there is hope in moving forward to create a better life that is full of love and joy. Continuing to react to your environment to whatever comes up next will only keep the wheel spinninig round and round in the same pattern. The trick is to take control of your thoughts, actions, and deeds in order to change your life's direction where you really want it to be. Easier said than done! It's not important where you start out, but the decisions you make about where you're determined to end up that matters! Your life <u>WILL</u> change the moment you make a committed decision. Use that incredible force that lies deep within you. You have to muster the courage to find it, and see it through to the end. Making mistakes will always occur in your life, but it will be what you do with those mistakes that will determine the direction life will take. Failure is a part of success in everybody's life. I am willing to say that every single successful person today met with many personal failures in their lives. Failing can be your motivating factor to strive to do better next time. It is ultimately your decision on what you want to do with that failure. Will you let it define you? Will you let it keep you at a level you are not happy with? Or will today be the day you finally decide that who you are as a person is much more than what you are currently living?

Will today be the day you decide once and for all to make your life everything you've always dreamed it would be? Ask yourself, "What will I do for myself today? What small step can I take today that will help myself make my tomorrow a better place?" Remember that big journeys begin with small steps! Take the first one today.

Most people are paralyzed by the fear that they don't know exactly how to turn their dreams into a reality. "Where do I even start?" They get stuck and in the end, never make that very important decision that would take them to a place they never knew existed. Instead, they remain in their comfort zone, a place that doesn't require much effort. Remember that as long as you stay sitting on that couch, nothing in your life will change. Nothing. Don't be that person. Just move and keep on moving forward. On the ladder of life, there are only two ways to go, either up or down. Remaining on the same step isn't an option. Fight for yourself because no one else will and that is the very sad truth. Only <u>YOU</u> can do it. I truly hope you make the decision to take a chance and invest in yourself. It will be the best thing you will ever do in life! I did it and it has changed my life forever! Not just my life, but all those around me because they benefit from the positive ripple effect that extends from the center of my being spreading miles around. All that I do in turn affects all those around me whether it be good or bad.

What I have learned in my personal journey of recovery is this: You have to teach others how to treat you. Only *you* can allow others to treat you with the respect you deserve. Remember, what you tolerate will continue. Look for those who will stand beside you in the rainy days and stay close to them. Don't let people take advantage of you just because you love them or they say they love you. The word love is used recklessly in these days and you must ask yourself do they truly know the meaning of love? Do You? I thought I did until I met my husband. He has shown me over and over the real meaning of what it is to love someone unconditionally. Stay away from those who say they love you one day, but mistreat you the next. That is not love. The word "sorry" is just as easily overused. Let actions, not words show you how they really feel. Tell yourself you deserve better than that. Step away from all gossip; if you start to hear people gossiping, walk away from that negativity. If they are talking about someone else behind their back, be guaranteed they are talking about you behind yours. You don't need those kinds of people in your life; they will drain you of your precious energy. Choose well who you surround yourself with. Live your life on your own terms and create something new and exciting in your life. Toxic people are all around us; learn to read the people around you and it will save you heartache in the long run. Look out for the negative people who will drain your power and bring out the worst in you. If you really want to change, you will need to press delete on some people and situations in your life, or spend as little time as possible around them. Don't answer to them, and do not let yourself feel guilty about it for one second, regardless if they are family. Take a time out from them. Surround yourself with people who will guide your steps in a positive way; people who will uplift you and support your decisions. Like Les Brown says, "If you are the smartest one in your group, you need a new group!" Stand strong in your own truth and don't be afraid to be different.

Most importantly, SPEND YOUR VALUABLE TIME ON YOU! You will become more peaceful and positive and will be able to think more clearly. YOU ARE THE VERY SOLUTION TO YOUR OWN PROBLEMS! Before you diagnose yourself with depression or low self-esteem, first make sure that you are not, in fact just surrounded by people whose main objective in life is to bring you down.

Know in your heart that you are simply ENOUGH! You are good enough, smart enough, beautiful enough, talented enough and most definitely strong enough! Believe it and never let insecurity and society's perception on how you should run your life change your attitude toward your own reflection and personality. Approve of yourself; learn to love yourself exactly the way you are. Don't let the five passions of the mind hold you prisoner. These are: Anger, Lust, Greed, Vanity and Attachment. Instead, let your life be ruled by the five virtues of the mind. These are: Discrimination, Forgiveness/Tolerance, Detachment, Contentment and Humility. Hold yourself in the highest regard and let your Light Shine ever so brightly! You have a Divine Spark of Light inside of you that no one can ever take away from you. Find it and nourish it back to life. No one is in charge of your happiness but you. It took me a very long time to learn that no would save me but myself. I only accomplished that because I had to learn the hard way that I, and only I, was the best person suited to look out for myself. The more you depend on yourself, the more positive control you have on EVERY aspect of your life. Take personal responsibility for who you are, what you do, and how you live. Most definitely do not allow another person to control your decisions regarding you or your life; this includes family, friends, and spouses. All I can say is KEEP THE FAITH! The best is yet to come. Today is only the beginning of the rest of your life. Keep moving forward in spite of your fears or insecurity of what the future holds. Use all your knowledge and skills you acquired so far in life to help you succeed on whatever path you choose. Believe that you can do anything you set your mind to and that it's POSSIBLE!

I am going to leave you with one last important true story. It is the story of the eagle. It can live up to 70 years, but to reach this age, the eagle must make a hard decision. In its 40th year, its long and flexible talons can no longer grab prey. Its long and sharp beak becomes bent. The feathers become old, thick and heavy. The thick & heavy feathers stick to its chest & makes it difficult to fly. Then, the eagle is left with only two options: DIE or go through a painful process of CHANGE. The process requires that the eagle fly to a mountaintop and sit on its nest. Then the eagle knocks its beak against a rock until it plucks out. It will wait for a new beak to grow back and then it will pluck out its talons. When its new talons grow back, the eagle starts plucking its old-aged feathers so new ones can grow back. A necessary Change that is worth sustaining. Afterwards, it takes its famous flight of rebirth and lives for 30 more years. Why is change needed? **To Survive and Live!** We too have to start the change process. Similar to the eagle, we also have to pluck out our unpleasant memories, negative habits, and fixed mindset. Only when we are freed from past burdens can we take advantage of the present. In order to take a new journey ahead in the future, let go of your negative old self-limiting beliefs. Open up your fixed mindset and fly like an eagle!

The eagle does not fight the snake on the ground. It picks it up into the sky and changes the battleground then it releases the snake into the sky. The snake has no stamina, no power and no balance in the air. It is useless, weak and vulnerable unlike on the ground where it is powerful wise and deadly. Take your fight into the spiritual realm where your Higher Power, the Universe, God or whomever it is you look to, will take over your battles and help you fight. Don't fight the enemy in his comfort zone; change the battleground like the eagle and let the Universe take charge of your problems. It works wonders when you are able to fight life's problems from a different perspective. Try it sometime.

In the end, let your Light shine bright so that others can see their way out of the dark. Remember that most days, you have to create your own sunshine! Be your own Lighthouse and show the way out of the darkness for others that may be on the verge of being swallowed by dark waters. You need to take care of yourself, love yourself, and forgive yourself as well as others around you, because we are all on the same journey called life; just at different levels of consciousness.

Remember:

- Look up, you'll see the sky
- Look down, you'll see the ground
- Look for anger and you'll find it
- Look for joy and you will be surrounded by it
- Look for fear and find it staring back at you
- Look for hope and feel its warm embrace
- Look within yourself and you will find Divine Love!

Ultimately you decide where to look, so WHERE ARE YOU GOING TO LOOK TODAY?

- I started a work boot recycling program during the first year at work when I saw all the boots being thrown away and still in good condition. I remembered before I started Women Building Futures I didn't have the money to buy boots in order to begin the program. This was a huge barrier to my golden opportunity to change my life for the better. It was the one thing I needed the most to get into the program and I didn't have the money to buy them. A girl I know found out I needed a pair of boots, and she gladly gave them to me. That random act of kindness gave me the chance to change my life. Fast forward to a year later, when I saw the large number of boots being thrown away, I immediately thought of all the struggling people who could use those boots. I went to the mine manager and requested starting a boot recycling program. He readily agreed and had 2 wooden bins built for me instead of my little cardboard box. To date I have well over 1700 pairs of boots that have been collected and distributed to local Safety Programs, that offer free safety tickets to those who cannot afford them. Then I come along with the boots and now people have the chance at finding a better paying job. The gratitude in their eyes only reflects what was in mine 5 years ago. I understand and am happy to be able to be a channel to aid them on their journey. What local charities are in your area that could use whatever help it is you have to offer? Often people don't know what they can do, and the answer to that is: SHOW UP! You have two feet and a heartbeat...you can be useful to someone.

I leave you with a prayer that has worked countless small miracles in my life. When in times of distress or difficulties, sit down read it out loud, or even write it over and over as many times as you need to. You can sit in contemplation, repeat it slowly and it will certainly bring results. It will give you strength and an inner force to help you through your day. I have been saying this prayer since I was a teenager and it truly does work. Try it sometime and you will understand the power of prayer.

Show me Thy ways, O Sugmad*
Teach me Thy Path.
Lead me in Thy truth, and teach me;
On Thee do I wait all day.
Remember, O Beloved, Thy guiding light
And Thy loving care.
For it has ever been Thy will,
To lead the least of Thy servants to Thee!

~Lai Tsi~

---

* The term Sugmad is derived from the ancient Sanskrit language and means God

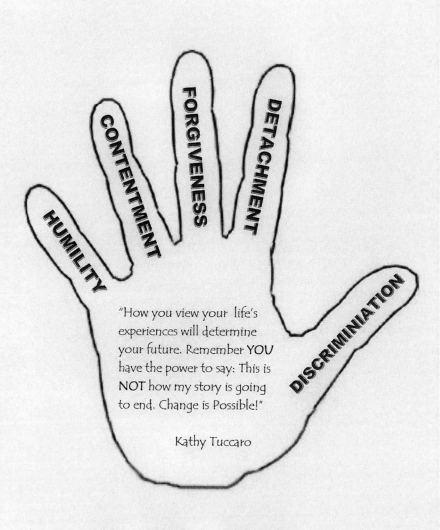

HUMILITY

CONTENTMENT

FORGIVENESS

DETACHMENT

DISCRIMINIATION

"How you view your life's experiences will determine your future. Remember YOU have the power to say: This is NOT how my story is going to end. Change is Possible!"

Kathy Tuccaro

Hand of Hope

Resources the Author Recommends

Klemp, Harold; HU – The Most Beautiful Prayer

Klemp, Harold; Beyond Meditation –
Spiritual Experiences Guidebook

Beattie, Melody; Codependent No More

Canadian Women Foundation website

Passion & willingness aren't always enough. I haven't been successful in every job I have run for. But I did learn from each experience. Don't give up because things get hard. Don't quit! If you believe in it, don't ever give up.

Bev Esslinger
City Councillor – Ward 2,
City of Edmonton, AB, Canada

The Artist

Evgeniya Kazimirskya, (known to most as Genia) was born in Minsk, Belarus in the Soviet Union era in 1982. She followed her grandfather's footsteps, who was a brilliant self-touched fine art painter. At the age of 10 she attended an art school under the Achremchik's National College of Art in Belarus. She graduated the college in 2000 from the faculty of monumental painting.

After immigrating to Canada in 2004, and reuniting with her father, she began painting and drawing again. Being inspired by the new country, Genia wanted to create the art she feared she forgotten how to do. Canada gave her a fresh start, unleashing her creativity and allowing her to utilize the skills taught by one of the best artists in Belarus! Genia has done close to a hundred of commissioned art work in the 11 years of living in Edmonton, Alberta. She has also owned & operated "No Cliche" gallery, where she was selling work from professional Belarussian artists.

Since 2016, she has earned the opportunity to withdraw from strictly commission work and be represented by a gallery. "This is a huge step forward for any artist! All we ultimately want is TIME to create" says Genia. She is currently working on various projects locally, but is expecting representation of her work in galleries throughout Canada. Proposals are currently being accepted. She can be reached at isidoraduncan@yahoo.ca or view her work on her website www.geniakazimirska.com

Little Warriors is a national, charitable organization committed to the awareness, prevention and treatment of child sexual abuse.

Little Warriors offers a free workshop called Prevent It! Taking Action to Stop Child Sexual Abuse to educate adults on how to help prevent child sexual abuse. The Little Warriors Be Brave Ranch is located east of Edmonton, AB and is the first of its kind long-term treatment centre for children ages 8-12 years old who have been sexually abused. To learn more visit www.littlewarriors.ca

221

The Author

Kathy Tuccaro's personal story of rising from the depths of homelessness to driving the biggest truck in the world, inspires many hurting Souls that anyone, anywhere and at any time can change their circumstances. She has fought her way through the dark times of losing everything, to discovering who she really was, and then completely transforming her life into one of success.

In addition to being a motivational speaker and Author, Kathy was a Nurse and worked on various Surgical/Medical/Geriatrics units for 13 years. She is also a certified Occupational Health & Safety Officer, and works full time as a Heavy Equipment Operator. She drives a

380+ ton (345 Metric Tonne), 797F Caterpillar Truck as well as a 208,000L water truck up in the Northern Alberta Oil Sands. She has always believed in dreaming bigger than the average population, and today she has proven it literally by driving "THE BIGGEST TRUCK IN THE WORLD!"

Her direct experience with violence, trauma and sexual abuse has given her much compassion, understanding, and wisdom for those wishing to take that important next step in the changing their destiny. Her passion for helping others develop a better self-worth has her travelling locally as well as internationally, to give personal development training at women's shelters, youth centers, recovery homes and schools.

Kathy was born in Val D'Or, Quebec, and speaks and writes fluently French and English. She is married and is a loving mother who lives in Edmonton, Alberta, Canada.